Motherhood in Black and White

By

ViAnn Prestwich

Motherhood in Black and White

Printed in the United States of America

Cover picture is William and Keeley Prestwich.

ISBN-13: 978-0692622933

ISBN-10: 0692622934

Paperback Edition: June 2016

Printed in the United States of America

Author's Forward

Family's timeline:

1985—Married

1990—Adopted Alexis

1992—Adopted Garrett

1994—Adopted Colton

1997—Adopted William

1997—Gave birth to Keeley

This is what our children looked like when I started this book and knew pretty much everything about parenting, sibling bonding and race relations.

From left to right William, Garrett, Alexis, Colton, Keeley

By the time they were this old, I knew a lot less. For Christmas, Colton gave us all these "Okayest" T-shirts, so, we got him one. From left to right, they are in the order of their birth: Alexis, Garrett, Colton, William and Keeley.

****

All of us say and do stupid things. What a sad world we would be living in if we forgot the good in individuals because we saw something stupid. For that reason, many of the names in this book have been changed. Most of the people who made insensitive statements shouldn't be remembered only for their indiscretions.

Praise for 'Motherhood in Black and White'

Four of ViAnn five children are adopted and one is not. Like Crayolas, the five range through colors from "peach" to dark brown, and the book tells the story of shepherding them through the years from birth to all grown up. Like every mother, adoptive or otherwise, ViAnn worries about how to "do it right." She struggles with the conflict between her simple - simple? - love for her kids and the esteem-challenging monkey wrenches that life, culture, and the community throw at her. It comes as no surprise that, in addition to the usual parenting issues, the mixture of the children's colors elicits gratuitous commentary from friends, relatives, and random passersby - commentary that (again, no surprise) ranges from the excruciatingly cruel to the breathtakingly dumb. But no need to rush to the author's defense. She takes it all on with an admirable equanimity that comes from her emotional steadiness together with the hanging-on-by-your-teeth that is the death-defying roller coaster of motherhood.

This book shines with the author's humanity, wisdom, and intelligence, along with a sly humor that made me laugh out loud several times on each page. Read it and be reassured that there is hope for the world after all.

- Joan Traub, New York Attorney/Writer. Mother of three grown daughters.

Years ago ViAnn opened her home to children —regardless of race. In these stories, she opens her home again to us and shares her journey of adoption and inter-family racial relations. Motherhood in Black and White provides a unique and equalizing microcosm of race relations. ViAnn uses her family's experiences as a backdrop for the emotions of both blacks and whites as well as adoptive parents and children.

While many might assert that race relations in the United States have regressed, ViAnn provides us opportunities to see additional possibilities of growth - provocatively and movingly presented. It is a journey that grows and matures in a compelling and persuasive way, and will take the reader along with it. And as she, at the end of the first chapter, makes a specific plea, we can hear a general one – will we, both black and white, overcome our fear, and help?

- Dr. Verl T. Pope, Professor of Counseling, Northern Kentucky University.

While reading this book I realized the insights offered in these pages aren't just for those who are raising children of difference races, they are for everyone. The author shares her story in an eye-opening and honest way, giving the reader an understanding of the unique challenges and rewards involved in raising a family of adopted children of different races. It's a compelling read, complete with humor, introspection, and a way of looking kindly past the foibles of others and choosing to remain positive and loving - a wonderful message for everyone.

- L. Whiting, Adoptee and Public Relations and Career Specialist

Follow our blog or go to our website at

http://www.krpublishing.org/

If you have any other thoughts, comments or ideas, feel free to post them on our website in the link above.

Table of Contents

Motherhood
in
Black & White

Chapter 1

When Colton called at 12:30 in the morning, he slurred his words and made little sense.

He had been living with my sister's family in an upper middleclass neighborhood a few miles outside of Salt Lake City, Utah: not exactly the diversity capital of the world. I answered the phone from our home in Washington State.

The Utah night was icy and bitter. This is a fact I was aware of because just four hours earlier, Colton and his father had been talking about the weather and how the frigid temperatures were affecting a construction project our son was helping with.

"Mom," he said as I fumbled awake at the sound of panic in my son's voice. "I can't pay for the car." He started to cry.

"Colton! What?" Adrenaline woke me fully.

“The tire’s off. It exploded maybe.” He sounded confused. “Maybe I hit the barrier.”

“Where are you?” I asked. For years, I had asked him where he was going and when he would be back, but he was no longer a teenager. I wasn’t exactly privy to his schedule.

“I was sick, so I left Nicole’s,” he told me and started to cry again. “I’m so cold. My head hurts. I’m so cold.” He hiccupped with a sob and then berated himself. His speech was difficult to understand. He rambled about being a Marine. “Marines don’t cry. And the lights keep coming. And they wouldn’t stop. Lights hurt you. I’m so cold.”

“Where are you?” I asked. I’d flipped a laptop open searching for a phone number to call the Sandy City police station. As soon as he told me his location, I would send someone to help him.

“I’m okay,” he slurred. “My head hurts. I’m so cold.”

“Where are you?” I tried again. “Are you off the road?”

“The lights keep coming,” he said.

“Where are you?” If I kept repeating myself, would he finally answer? My child, who typically wore dark clothes, was he stumbling along an icy, shadowy road, his car smashed on the barrier?

“My head hurts. I’m so cold,” I could hear him shiver and swallow his own sobs. “I think I was getting a fever at Nicole’s. Now the tire’s gone.”

“Are you with your car?” I asked.

“The tire is gone,” he cried.

A few years earlier I had watched him duck his head and wipe a tear when his 4 X 100 relay team got disqualified at state track competition. But other than the state championships, I had not seen or heard him weep since third grade when a kid on the bus told him black people caused most of the violence in the “whole world.”

“Where are you?”

"In a parking lot now?" His voice shivered in the arctic air. Most of his rambling was incoherent. "My head hurts so bad."

"Did you hit your head?"

"Ooh, it hurts."

"Where are you? I'll send someone to help you."

"No. Don't call. I'm okay," he sounded pathetic. "I'm scared," he whispered. "I can't cry."

There was nothing for me to do except fearfully listen and beg him to tell me where he was.

The phone must have dropped. For a long time all I heard were unidentifiable noises.

After wandering the living room worrying about my son that night, I decided to finish this manuscript. Five chapters have sat for nearly a decade unread and untouched. I didn't want to examine what I had written. Something about the stories bothered me. The incidents are true. I've left out anything too embarrassing. Why then could I not revisit this work and let others read about our happy biracial family?

Finally, I realized what disturbed me. Every time I started reading I would remember Carol's comments. Carol was a good friend and writer. I'd wanted her to see if anything I'd written was worth publishing. She had perused a few pages and said, "It sounds like you think people treat your family differently because you have black kids. Like there is a lot of prejudice around. And I just don't see it."

At the time, several years ago, I was reluctant to put our cute little story of black and white kids bonding in a home, out into the world. I didn't want to add to the clamor of the victims' chorus: "Someone hurt my feelings, poor me."

In reality, our life was wonderful. I didn't want anyone to think I was presenting a "Woe is me," scenario. So many people would react like Carol, saying, "I see very little prejudice."

Then there are those on the other end of the spectrum who intimately know about the existence of intolerant behavior. The individuals, who, if by some miracle happened upon this story, would read my family's cute little escapades of using real Clorox to put out pretend campfires in the living room and feel we aren't concerned enough about the blatant as well as covert prejudice surrounding us. This latter group does not see our family as "cute."

If Carol felt the general population was being maligned by the hint of prejudice, this other group feels even more strongly the need to protect a black child from white parents who couldn't ever understand black culture or how it feels to be black.

"Love isn't enough," I have been told. "You can't love him enough to compensate for the white privileged attitude you have."

As I wandered through the living room on a bitterly, cold night worrying about my son, an incoherent black kid in a dark parking lot of an unfamiliar city, I decided to add to the clamor. Because whether you or I want to accept the fact, my son's situation was made more complicated because of his skin. And you out there who tell me love isn't enough: Well, it's all I have. And when he dropped into our lives over 20-years ago, I was all he had. So both of you—you who don't recognize prejudice and you who feel we should never have attempted to raise him--could we agree adoption issues, especially those involving biracial adoptions, have few absolutes.

While I begged my mumbling black son to read me some sign from a building or the road, I was angry at you both--you who don't believe he is in more danger than a lighter-skinned man and you who would say he is in more danger because he wasn't taught by a black man how to deal with this situation.

Mostly, I wondered if anyone would see him and stop. I wondered if he would freeze to death ten feet from a freeway. Would he go unconscious as his brain swelled with a concussion? Who would help him? Who would fear him?

Would he give them reason to fear him? Like most boys, Colton didn't always make logical decisions. Especially under duress. He was only 10 years old when he appeared to threaten a football referee. That was the year I noticed how he swaggered and strutted if he managed to tackle an opponent or carry a football across the goal line. Self-satisfaction would ooze right through those foul-smelling pads. During a game, he was like many competitors and held firm to the belief football actually matters to the preservation of mankind.

On that particular fall day, Colton was a fourth grader and had managed to catch a pass. While some overzealous mothers screamed, my son dodged through enough defensive players to score just before being tackled to the ground. This success overloaded his body with enough crazy chemicals so that he felt no pain, and certainly he was too busy strutting around bumping pads with the other heroes on the field to notice any rearrangement of his first digit.

The coaches sent a runner in with the play, and the team settled into formation for a two-point conversion attempt.

"I looked down," Colton explained to me later, "and my thumb was in the wrong place."

Both of his feeble attempts to flip the first metacarpal back into place failed. This was of enough concern to the 10-year-old, he decided he probably wasn't the most capable offensive player to carry the ball on the upcoming play. Had the coaches ever discussed this particular situation in practice? Colton couldn't remember. Certainly, they had suggested a hurt player should lie on the ground so the referees would call a timeout, but Colton felt fine. The problem wasn't pain, the problem was the thumb had somehow flipped over and migrated toward the wrist. More to the point, the inexperienced player wasn't sure flopping to the turf just as the quarterback was readying to receive the snap would give the other players enough warning to "take a knee." Still, his unmanageable thumb just didn't seem capable of clinging to a ball and surging through a defensive line.

Making a snap decision, Colton spun and moved toward the sideline. An observant referee threw a penalty flag. In an attempt to explain the predicament, Colton waved his right hand and rushed toward the official. Now starting to feel pain, his face and raised fingers apparently looked a bit threatening and another yellow flag flew.

After a short discussion, the officials decided there would be no penalties. It's hard to call a 15-yard personal foul on a kid who is apologizing for his errant thumb.

If someone stopped for Colton on this cold night, would he rush toward them? How many young black men had been shot because they looked threatening?

Would someone care enough to overcome fear and help my black child?

Chapter 2

Nearly two decades before the night my son called with reduced functions due to a spiked fever and a head injury, I gave birth for the first time. This wasn't our first child. There were already four in our home, demanding food, demanding attention, and refusing to sleep with any regularity.

Neighbors, mothers, midwifery kind of people, and women who adored breastfeeding were quick to say how lucky I was to finally "have one of my own" as if we were just renting the others. People have insinuated, sometimes rudely insinuated, I would never really know love until I had "one of my own." Were they right?

With all these comments, I even began to wonder if I would feel differently about this child. A few weeks after she was born, I was on the couch holding her. I searched her tiny little face. She lay lightly in the crook of one arm. For nine months, I had carried her under my heart. Every gene she carried had been provided by either my husband or myself. Did I love her more?

I looked at her skin, colored like her father's. I looked at her hair, soft and tinted like mine. I looked at the perfect hands, tiny pink fingernails.

Slumped next to us on the couch was 3-year-old Colton. He'd fallen slightly forward and was practically sleeping in the book I had been reading him. His soft breath stopped as he pulled his silky blanket around his cheek and settled more comfortably against my side.

I could see the back of his neck, the darkest part on him. Alexis, our oldest child, had been 4 when we'd flown to Colorado and picked this little guy up. She'd watched me lay him in the tub.

"He's brown all over," she said, a little surprised.

I tried to explain how his nationality is African and that he is called black just like she is considered white.

"He's not black," Alexis said secure in her recently acquired knowledge of colors. "He's brown."

"Yes," I admitted, "but . . ." I was trying to think of a way to explain when she continued rather condescendingly.

"And I'm not white," she looked at her arm. "I'm brown, too. He's dark brown; I'm light brown." She was pleased to have figured something out which her mother didn't even understand. For a long time she refused to allow anyone to call her little brother black.

Nevertheless, that afternoon, as I sat on the couch with two of my children, the back of my son's neck was closer to black than brown. The summer sun had darkened him. While settling him more comfortably on my leg, I could feel how dry his curls were. He needed some hair lotion on them. I looked at the dark line his long lashes made as he slept. His nose was flat. His hair curled tightly against his head. He looked nothing like my husband or me.

Again, I watched my little girl. Never had I thought I would produce something so beautiful. Yes, her eyes were like her father's. Her mouth like her aunt's. Did I love her? Yes, an incredible amount. Her solemn little eyes looked up.

Did her biological connection create in me a stronger bond than I had for the little guy slumbering next to me?

I picked up one of his sturdy hands. The long dark fingers were tipped light where the fingernails covered skin as fair as my own. Turning his hand over, I studied the pale palm in contrast to the dark back.

Years ago, a man at the restaurant where I worked told me a joke about those white palms.

"Why do black people have white palms?" he'd asked. (Not really using the term "black" but a derogatory name.) "Hey, bro, give me five," the man demonstrated, slapping hands in an energetic high five. "They wore the color right off."

Years later an African-American friend told me the same witticism, only he said that the palms were light because the "black was worn off from hard work."

I squeezed my son's hand as I thought of the things those little hands did every day. Sometimes they did participate in energetic high fives, mostly at the grocery store with "light brown" bag boys who said, "Yo, bro," while playing with him in the cart. Nevertheless, those little hands worked hard, too. Why just that morning they had held him stable as he climbed the refrigerator racks to the top shelf and thrown down a gallon of milk, an economy size bottle of ketchup, and a tub of margarine. He was looking for "good juice," as opposed to the Kool-aide I'd served him in a sippy cup. He preferred fresh squeezed orange juice or at least frozen concentrate. A couple days earlier he had worked hard to fill the oven with Tupperware bowls, a fact I didn't notice until it was nearly preheated enough for pot pies.

I turned his hand over again and looked at the ink which had settled in the cracks of his palms. He'd helped me make newspaper hats. None of which would stay on his ever bobbing little head. Love flooded through me.

After so many miscarriages, Keeley's first kick was only a warning of what might be potential grief. Mornings when I threw up and nights when I slept in a chair were greeted with hope not justified by doctors' predications. Still, ultrasounds showed normal growth, so I endured swollen legs, backaches, and limited mobility with gratitude that I was having the experience of producing a child. The delivery was complicated. Because of the cesarean birth, my first glimpse of her blurred. During the hospital stay and recovery time, I was vaguely curious. Would I have a connection with this child that I lacked with my others? Would I feel a stronger bonding, a closer connection to this biological child of mine?

Was my love for the infant I carried, the infant I gave genetic material to, stronger than my love, dedication and devotion to the four children we had adopted?

Would my biological daughter love me more than the children I adopted love me? Sensational talk shows and articles have left their impression on my psyche. I punished myself by reading and watching reunion stories of mothers who placed children for adoption. Stories of children who spend incredible amounts of time and emotional energy to find "real" mothers. Is biology so strong to bind people more than days and years of association? All the reunion stories seemed to say "yes," that the life experiences I had with my children were nothing compared to the biological bond.

What kind of relationship my children choose to have with their biological family will be up to them. I will support them and encourage them in their desires. But before I could welcome other family entities,

I had to know what biology meant to me. I had done motherhood both ways now. I had adopted. I had given birth. I had adopted white. I had adopted black.

I wanted to be honest with myself and in a quiet moment I realized one thing. They are none of them my own, all only on loan from God. I loved all my children. They exasperated me differently. They demanded different disciplines and time. But my affection for them was the same. The little pink stranger now sleeping against my chest and the dark brown child snoring softly against my leg--I felt connected to, protective of, and love for them both. And the other three that, for the moment, were out of sight, I loved them just as much. They belonged to our circle called family.

The days and the years since our daughter's birth have done nothing but strengthen our love and dedication to each of our children. Sometimes I want to insinuate how people won't know true love, real love until they have felt this deep an emotion for someone not "their own," until they feel love for someone "unlike" themselves. But I don't do that. It would be rude.

Chapter 3

As newlyweds, Clare and I had planned on having children, several or a few depending on our abilities. We tried and did not succeed. Two surgeries later we were informed that children probably never would come. So we adopted a blue-eyed infant who looked like her father. Beautiful she was. Beautiful. A child we were more than proud of. I glowed every time someone said, "You can tell she belongs to them; she looks just like her father. She was certainly meant to be in your home."

We had indeed been matched with a child that "fit" our family. As we read letters from the birthmother and her family, we came to love them and knew what wonderful people they were. The child was a fitting addition to our family. Later, when we applied to adopt another child, I, of course, knew the next one would look just like us, too. He would make another visible reminder that he was a child meant to be in our home.

"He's my son and I'm going to go get him," said my husband after we'd heard about a little boy who needed a home.

"I'm not sure." I'd been uncertain for several reasons. Not so much because he was part black, but because he wouldn't look like us. And then how would we know he was supposed to be with us? How would we know to love him? Could we love him? I'd never really loved someone that wasn't like me. Oh, sure, a Korean roommate in college, and some Native Americans, but love him for eternity?

We did love him. The stocky kid with wavy hair and a deep tan. And within days, Garrett's black part was just part of him, and I completely loved him. Some extended family weren't quite so quick to accept a "Negro." An in-law told at least one curious person our son was "part Tongan."

We didn't care much what was said. We were a family--a family with a tanned baby. We felt blessed beyond our comprehension. We had the children that we thought we'd never have.

"You shouldn't put kids in walkers. They're dangerous," Paula explained this to me as she brushed one fingertip along a scab on Garrett's cheek. "Just saying."

A week earlier, the 9-month-old who couldn't quite walk, had been energetically strolling around the house encased in a "dangerous" baby walker. For a while, the already social little guy would stand in the living room near the heavy picture window. Anytime people walked by, Garrett would pound with an open palm trying to get their attention. When pedestrian traffic was slow, he'd turn his four-wheeled vehicle to the kitchen and raise his pudgy hands toward the graham cracker cabinet. Armed with a fresh cracker, he'd returned to smear another coat of slime on the window. During one of his frequent trips, a wheel had caught the molding and toppled him onto the carpet.

As Paula lectured about baby walkers, Garrett smiled cheerfully, unconcerned with the grilling I was receiving. His pleasant disposition was hard to resist.

"I feel so bad for his mother," Paula continued. "She'll never get to see him laugh or grow up. How does that make you feel, knowing all the pain she's going through?"

"Uh," I stammered.

"Just asking," Paula raised an eyebrow. "Doesn't it make you feel selfish taking her child?"

"Uh," I stammered.

"Just asking."

"I just want to give a good home . . ." I stammered.

"How do you know you're equipped to do so?"

Paula wasn't the first or the last to suggest adopting a child was selfish—selfish and arrogant. Selfish to take someone's child and arrogant to think we know the best way to raise this child.

Selfish and arrogant. The title haunted me. I wasn't selfish. Was I? I wasn't arrogant. Was I?

Adoption is a complicated, intrusive process not for the timid or faint of heart. Couples who adopt must be prepared to have their home measured, assessed. Financial records, background checks and work history all become part of a large file. Classes dealing with adoption are usually required. Some of the instructors know what they are talking about; others have watched too many talk shows. Going to an adoption group was a painful, sweet experience. The social worker involved in the adoption of our first two children, tried hard to make the meetings a worthwhile experience. Typically, he would have birth mothers who had recently placed children talk about their experiences. The stories we heard there are not for my telling, but they were compelling, heart-rending stories of girls who knew what they had to do. I knew if my children could inherit anything from their birth parents, I wanted it to be the strength I saw in these girls.

Each meeting also featured parents who had new babies. I watched one couple get up holding their beautiful infant. The father spoke first, telling how this child had come after a four or five or twenty year wait. His narrative about waiting is rather vague in my mind, but I do remember what he said next. He spoke poignantly to all the ones like my husband and me who were still waiting.

"I want to tell all of you that are waiting. Now that we have our child, the pain seems like it was only for a moment. It is all worth it and the waiting made getting our child even sweeter."

I listened carefully to his words and thought, "I hate you."

After we got each of our children, they asked us to speak at a meeting. I got up and said how grateful I was for the birthparents who placed this child with us, and I was humbled at the responsibility. Both statements sounded the opposite of selfish and arrogant. What I had wanted to say was exactly what the new father had said about the pain seemingly like only a moment. But I didn't. I didn't want everyone to hate me.

Chapter 4

For several weeks I'd been following the atrocities occurring in Africa. Horrible stories about women searching mass graves for loved ones. The searchers held scarves up to their faces to protect themselves from the awful smell. The pictures always invoked a kind of detached pity and sympathy in me. I couldn't understand how a people could be so horrible to another people. I read with vague grief about people starving. I studied pictures of malnourished children staring big-eyed into cameras aimed at their suffering but offering no help.

I sat one day in my comfortable home and wondered what could be done, then flipped the paper to find "Dear Abby". On the back page was a picture of two border patrol guards from the UN. Between them stood a boy. "An unknown orphan boy" the caption explained. The boy could have been three, four or five. Skinny, with ragged shorts, he was eating a crust of bread which, according to the caption, one of the border guards had given him. Unlike the other pictures I'd viewed, this picture didn't invoke detached feelings. My inner core hurt with the little boy's pain. I felt fear for his plight. I sat in my chair and cried.

I showed the picture to my husband and said that if I knew how or where I'd go get this little boy. I cut the photo out and stuck it in a desk drawer. Periodically, I'd stir through the drawer for something and see this picture. I'd receive a weird jolt. The jolt was enough to motivate us to become foster certified in case there was a child who needed a place to stay.

The caseworker was abnormally cheerful when he called to tell us about a 9-week-old baby who needed a different foster home. We would be his third. Really? How much trouble can a healthy newborn be?

"He is one of our more high-maintenance babies," the voice on the other end of the phone said cheerfully. "He has a rather delicate digestive system."

An examination of that statement is in order about now. Astute homebuyers know all real estate ads have a few code words.

If, for example, the ad says the home is "cozy," an intelligent reader knows this means the rooms are so tiny you have to breathe in to get past the furniture. If the home is described as, "needing TLC," you may freely substitute "OMG" for "TLC." A home described as "energy efficient" probably has a clothes line in the back yard. The ad says "retro décor." Can you say '60s flashback, paisley vinyl floors and avocado appliances?" Groovy.

"Close-knit community" means nosy neighbors. "Motivated seller" could imply nasty neighbors.

Social workers have a few of their own "code" words. "Delicate digestive system," means the child has colic so bad the screaming requires closed windows so the neighbors won't call social services. Or maybe "delicate digestive system" means projectile vomiting and within a few days every surface in your home will smell like spoiled cottage cheese.

In our case, "high-maintenance baby" meant we wouldn't get three straight hours of sleep for another three years. He'd be a pre-teen before sleeping five hours in a row. And once he was a teenager, we'd really start becoming sleep deprived. Of course, sleep deprivation during his teen years had nothing to do with his "delicate digestive system."

Legally the child was not available for adoption because the courts were looking for a birth father. Still, the foster home he was in could not deal with him. One of the foster mothers explained, "I've had hundreds of infants, and I thought I knew what high maintenance meant," she said using a favorite code word, "But this little guy. Whoa." (Whoa is a code word for "we need some additional descriptive code words.")

Our destination to pick up Colton was a new connection for the airline we flew on. The grand opening was still being celebrated with stale doughnuts at the loading gates and sagging helium balloons. Seating was plentiful with only about six other passengers. We carried an empty baby seat expecting to fill it for the return flight. There were four experienced flight attendants instructing four inexperienced flight attendant trainees. Our oldest, Alexis, was 4 years old and Garrett was 2 years old when we flew out to pick Colton up. These two children got a warped view of what to expect from airline service. As soon as one child finished fish crackers a flight attendant was offering to open a peanut snack. As soon as one child spilt orange juice, another flight attendant was offering apple juice. Our trays were never in the upright position. And every flight attendant, both trainee and trainer, eyed the empty baby carrier occupying the aisle seat.

He was dark and he had curly hair. His skin was dry and starting to crack. I thought the poor little guy needed an attentive mother. The baby didn't appear to want one, however. He lay stiff and unresponsive as we tried to feed him. He wouldn't let me hold him close or cuddle him. He arched away and stared with intelligent eyes, memorizing this next set of caregivers.

The baby's new siblings appeared unconcerned with his color. Alexis was covetous of the little red and blue shoes the baby wore, and Garrett, who hadn't used a pacifier in six months, absconded with the one from the baby's mouth and energetically used it for the next year.

"How will we raise him?" I whined to my husband. "We need advice."

"He's our son," said Clare, "We'll raise him like that."

"But he's black."

"Yeah," Clare said, bored with the whole concept.

And for a long time, that is how my husband, the children's father, remained. Not bored with his children. He's fed them at 2:30 in the morning, balanced them on their hands and knees trying to teach them to crawl, delighted in their growth, laughed heartily as they wrestled on the floor, beamed proudly when they hammered large nails, bragged about every athletic accomplishment as if his genetic material produced the achievement, complained disgustedly when they filled the lawn mower tank with sand or experimented with the toilet's ability to dispose of Legos. The whole time he ignored comments about race. Some comments he never even understood because so seldom did he dwell on race or adoption.

He's flown dozens of red-eye flights to be home in time for football games, rugby matches, basketball games, band concerts and scout trips. Granted, he slept through most of the band concerts and complained about not sleeping during the scout trips, but still he was there when he could be.

In fact, when he read the first draft of this manuscript, he said, "Too many questions at the first of this. I never worried about any of that--loving one kid more or 'bonding.'"

Those who view us as unfit to parent because we are not biologically related or because we are of a different color would read the preceding and point out how Clare's insensitivity was detrimental to our children.

But what was he supposed to do, remind them weekly, monthly or on every birthday they were adopted? Was he supposed to introduce them as his "adopted" child?

He was supportive of our oldest daughter finding her birthmother. He didn't care if the "other mother" came to our daughter's wedding or even stood in line with us. He even joked about how, if this "other" mother wanted to feel more involved, she could pay for the transmission that just went out in Alexis' car.

As an engineer he had opportunities to travel to third-world countries. The kids weren't really fond of these trips because, upon his return, he was much less likely to purchase them anything.

Someone asking for an additional pair of shoes might get a lecture.

"How many shoes do you have? Your closet is full. All of them name brand. Do you know there are kids that don't have shoes?" he would ask. "Some of the kids I saw last week had cut up old tires and made sandals. They were wearing tires strapped to their feet."

"Seriously?" one of the boys asked.

"Name brand tires," Alexis nodded. "I'm sure they were wearing Michelin."

Of course, the day we picked up Colton, we didn't know these children would eventually feel specific logos made shoes more comfortable. Instead I was worried about how to raise this newest member of our family. All Clare wanted to do was sign the papers and hurry back to the airport for a return flight. I wanted to go visit with a family who had adopted three black children.

We spent a pleasant evening admiring their children and silently thinking, "Our baby's cuter than your baby."

Their two older children and our two older children played tag and spread toys across the bedroom floors. We listened to the more experienced couple relay encounters unique to biracial families.

"You get what you look for," was the final message the father left us with. "There will be good experiences and bad experiences. Whatever you are looking for is what you will find the most of."

"I know that," I thought. "That's all you can come up with to help us raise this little guy?"

For several years I had taught that exact principle to my students. I had the dubious honor of teaching the YIC kids, Youth In Custody. Their behavior warranted their custody status. They were an eclectic lot of ragtag youth who complained bitterly about the unfairness of the world. Early in the semester I'd take them on a tour of other classrooms. Divided into groups, they were asked to inspect the school as a sort of student advisory group. One body-pierced, weed-smelling group would wander through classrooms looking for damage to the ceiling. Another equally antisocial group would have been assigned to report on student destruction of the floors, a third was to watch for graffiti on the desks, still another was supposed to identify improvements which had been made in the old school.

After filling out official looking forms we returned to our classroom. The entire group was to come to a consensus as to where the majority of the district maintenance money should be spent. With few exceptions, those assigned to concentrate on the ceiling felt the ceiling was badly in need of repair. Those who watched for graffiti felt the majority of money should go toward new desks; and those who were concentrating on the floors argued fairly convincingly our walking surfaces were unsafe. The small group that was to look for improvements usually felt the school wasn't in such a bad shape.

Normally, after the discussion of how they each saw more of what they were looking for and found what they expected to see, we had to take a second tour of the school.

"You find what you expect to find," is what we were told by this adoptive father. "If you want to find the negative about racial adoption, it's out there, but most of what happens is positive. So enjoy your new son and dwell on the positive."

The return flight home had the same trainers and trainees. They fed peanuts to our children and prepared for the inevitable juice spills. This time they eyed the baby carrier with even more curiosity than before. One passenger openly stared at our new child. She followed us out of the terminal and then sat with us as we waited for a shuttle.

"Are you adopting that baby?" the woman asked. Her voice betrayed none of her racial values.

'Where is that darn shuttle," I thought irritably.

"My sister has adopted three black children," the woman continued. "I love those kids."

I was irritated when the shuttle came and ended our conversation about the woman's beautiful nieces.

Chapter 5

"What is he?" asked Candy. She leaned over the baby squirming amongst his soft blankets. She tentatively touched his dark brown cheek. The face was rough and scaling. My attention had not helped his skin. Around the little mouth and down his chin and neck, the dryness had become even worse. The skin was cracked and oozing blood. When he wasn't arching his back and hitting his head against our teeth because of his "digestive problem," he was bleeding.

Some girls where I taught had heard about our family adopting this 2-month-old infant. Bringing a blue quilt and other small presents, they had come to hold a soft, cuddly newborn.

I had always loved how teenage students treated the arrival of each of our babies. We had received tremendous amounts of support and assistance. When we got our oldest daughter, the young girls expressed delight over her delicate features, her wavy hair, and her soft skin. They declared her precious and wore her out with their attentions. When our second child had entered our home, visitors remarked what a strapping big boy he was and what a strong grip he had. With his handsome face, he would do great things.

Today, none of the girls peering down on my new son said he was cute. His skin was horribly affected with a disease we would fight for many months. His hair was patchy and full of scabs. Always scratching and squirming to get comfortable, he wasn't cuddly.

An awkward pause followed Candy's question. "What is he?" I should not have been offended by her query. Although tactlessly put, and spoken in the same tone one would ask about an exotic breed of rodent, she simply wanted to know his nationality.

My husband and I were more than willing to talk about our children's various origins. We wanted the kids to be proud of their heritages and grateful for the uniqueness of their beginnings. However, today I was fatigued. The baby woke several times a night digging at his face, trying to relieve the burning and agony he felt. I'd slather him with ointments and then forcefully hold his hands and feet so he would not worsen his infections. Finally, the tortured infant would become exhausted, and we would both sleep for two or three hours before his discomfort became so bad he would wake again.

"What is he?" I thought. "He's a child in pain."

"Where'd he come from?" asked another girl.

Abruptly, Sonny stepped forward and took my little boy. Sonny was Korean and as happy as her name. She bounced the baby, and then held him up in front of her so she could look into his face. The infant solemnly stared back at her. He had beautiful eyes, clear and alert. Eyes which appeared to understand more than he could communicate.

"He came from heaven," said Sonny cheerfully.

Unmindful of the infant's physical problems, Sonny talked into the little boy's eyes. Suddenly, I realized her confidence and love stemmed from knowing what she was and where she came from. She came from heaven, too.

***

People would often assume Colton's skin problem was a black thing and we were doing something wrong as white parents. Like maybe Southern fried grits would alleviate his rash or maybe he was having a psychosomatic reaction to losing his culture.

We saw doctors aplenty: white pediatricians, black pediatricians, an arrogant dermatologist who wouldn't actually touch the baby as well as a neighbor who sold naturopathic cures.

We bought two-ounce tubes of steroid cream for seventy dollars. We bought lotions with "solubilized coal tar extract" which made the baby scream. We bathed him in oatmeal and gave him so much Benadryl he became immune. We spent two thousand dollars on a water softener, washed his clothes in special detergent and slept very little.

Finally, we took him to a dermatologist at a children's hospital. She listened for a long time. She heard my theory about how he seemed to be worse when the air quality was poor and how his best period had been when I'd been taking him to a "mommy and me" swim class. Later she confirmed how they see a higher number of skin problems when inversions are mixed with a high level of pollutants. She also suggested chlorine in the swim water was fighting a secondary infection.

"Put a tiny bit of Clorox in his bath water," she advised. "It will work like the chlorine. See if that relieves some of the symptoms." The Clorox combined with several medicated ointments helped.

I was obviously boring my neighbors with our skin drama because one lady wasn't quite with me when I said, "And we put about a teaspoon of Clorox in his bath water."

She kind of woke up from an apathetic daze and said, "I don't think Clorox will help fade his pigment any. You're just going to have to accept him as he is."

Our extended families have accepted our children to various degrees. My grandmother was a refined woman who loved her grandchildren as much as she loved education. Her favorite chair was always surrounded by books. She was a spiritual woman who tried to live her religion and have compassion for all mankind. She had, however, been raised to believe some "mankind" was superior to other "mankind." She was from a generation who didn't sit in the same restaurant or in the same schools with a "Negro." Her religion and her culture had taught her to justify this segregation.

I don't know who told my grandmother about her new great-grandson. He was several months old before we met with her at a family gathering. Grandma hugged us and we visited. I saw her watching Colton's nappy head as he wiggled in his dad's arms. Finally, Grandma asked to hold him.

She tentatively propped him on her lap and tilted her head to one side watching him as he watched her. Eventually, she looked up and said. "I've never touched a black person before."

How she felt about this first experience was never mentioned in my presence.

Chapter 6

After we had Colton for a while, I'd forgotten to look for prejudices or stereotypes. We had three little kids. I had other obligations, and life was just plain too busy to keep track of who said what. If it hadn't been for the man's subdued laughter, the woman in the bank would have just seemed a bit eccentric.

The drive-up window had a long line, so I foolishly decided to take three preschoolers into the bank. Unstrapping them from their car seats and assembling them so they could safely cross the parking lot was a feat of crowd control. Immediately upon entering the lobby, the older two were occupied with trying to shake candy out of the candy machines. The machines were those top-heavy affairs with candy enclosed in a glass bubble.

"Please, don't shake those," I said sweetly aware of the quiet people around me. "We wouldn't want them to fall on your heads and break." I could picture shattered glass and cheap lemon drops spread across the high traffic areas. Going over to tell them to stop would have required I leave a barely walking toddler to hold my place in line and worse would have resulted in a public power struggle. The two children were now turning the knobs trying to force the contraption to work without a quarter. I shook my head, hoping no one would know they were with me and tried to write my check while holding Colton. A woman behind us, probably a pillar in her community as well as her church, pushed out a professionally manicured peach fingernail and barely touched my son's tight curls.

"I bet he likes to dance," she commented.

"Uh, yeah," I said, spelling forty with a "u."

An elderly oriental man was in line just in front of us and was discretely watching my disarray. I saw him quickly eye the woman behind me taking note of her elegant grey hair, rhinestone ear rings, and expensive wool coat. He smiled and once again faced the bank tellers.

At the same time my older two decided to check under the machines for stray candy. All I could see were their little rear ends. I put Colton on the floor and tried to make the "u" look like an "r" in the word forty.

"I'll bet he's got rhythm," said the woman, once again carefully touching Colton's hair in the same manner one might poke at a dead spider.

My other two were now kneeling on the floor triumphantly holding a couple slightly damaged gum balls. With my sternest mother look, I waved them over. They sidled up just as the lady started singing.

"I've got rhythm, I've got rhythm, I've got rhythm." She snapped her figures awkwardly in time to the only line she knew from the song. She swayed slightly trying to encourage Colton to dance. "I've got rhythm, I've got rhythm."

The oriental man's shoulders shook with laughter. Only then did

I understand what the woman meant. She started again to sing, "I got rhythm, I got rhythm," the same line over and over. My black toddler eyed her warily, totally unimpressed with her attempt at rhythm. (For the record, she had none.) My little girl tried to imitate the finger snapping. Garrett offered the woman a gum ball.

***

More often than not, the comments weren't motivated by bigotry but dealt mostly with stereotypes. "You'll need a basketball standard for sure," said one neighbor, referring to how all blacks everywhere play basketball.

"I suppose you eat a lot of watermelon," a fruit stand operator told me one summer. "Well, I do," I told her, paying for two watermelons and a cantaloupe. "But he hates it," I said motioning to Colton, "except the part about rolling it out of the van onto the concrete. He likes that."

A 16-year-old babysitter once told me she couldn't wait until our little boy started talking. "Little black boys sound so cute. Like that kid on the cereal commercial." Weeks later I finally saw the commercial she was referring to. The kid's Southern accent was appealing but to my untrained ear, it sounded just like the little blonde boys from Alabama and my Aunt Wilma.

Colton has always disliked chocolate. A concept foreign to someone like me, who is addicted to chocolate-covered almonds. But from his earliest days, he has not wanted to have anything to do with chocolate. He wouldn't drink chocolate milk. Even as an infant, he spit out chocolate pudding or ice cream. He would meticulously pick the chocolate chips out of cookies and leave them on the carpet where they melted, were stepped on, or simply appeared as suspicious foreign matter.

"Just eat them," I pleaded. "They're good."

"You like them?" he asked.

"They're really good." From then on, he graciously saved them in a sweaty palm and presented them to me as a present.

"You can eat these," he smiled as he kindly thrust deformed chocolate lumps in my face.

Gloria Tatton introduced herself soon after we started going to her church. She had explained how her family used to live next door to a single mother who had a couple "darker children."

"It was one of those situations," Gloria said lowering her voice.

I watched her blankly, wondering about "those situations" producing "those darker children."

Gloria continued. "I used to tell my own children how they were white like vanilla and those other children were dark like chocolate. And we all love chocolate, don't we? I think my kids got the message."

Now she was proving how much she loved chocolate by tentatively rubbing my son's head and saying, "You're just a little chocolate boy."

In the middle of the crowded foyer, Colton dropped to the floor. He laid his head on the well-traveled carpet and cried like only a three-year-old can.

"I'm not a chocolate boy," he sobbed. "Mom, I don't want to be a chocolate boy."

People stopped gossiping and watched. Mothers quit hurrying toward the parking lot and gasped as the little boy wiped his running nose with a clenched fist and begged me. "Mama, I don't want to be a chocolate boy."

"He'll have to learn to accept his coloring someday," the woman said sadly.

"For Pete sakes," I wanted to tell the lady. "Call him mud face, if you want. He likes mud. At this age he could care less what his color is. He just doesn't like chocolate."

"Shut up, cry baby," his older brother said in disgust.

The only thing Colton hated worse than chocolate was being called a cry baby. He sat up quickly and punched at Garrett's leg, "I'm not a cry baby!"

"Are too! Cry baby!"

At this, Colton stood up and swung angrily. "I'm not a cry baby and I'm not a chocolate boy." We hauled the two brothers out to the car to continue their argument.

The same good woman who insisted she liked chocolate kids was over at the house one day. Colton was sitting at the bottom of the stairs. He was clutching a thick coil of nylon rope to his chest like a security blanket and crying softly.

"What's wrong," Gloria asked sympathetically. Her question produced a fresh round of tears. Colton looked at her quickly and then buried his tear-streaked face back into the carpeted step.

"He's upset because I wouldn't let him use his George George George of the Jungle swing."

The little boy stopped crying and was listening appreciatively to my explanation. "He knots a rope, kid style, around the stair railing and then around his ankle. He wants to climb to the top of the banister and jump to swing like George of the Jungle," I finished.

"I guess swinging from vines is kind of inborn," she observed seriously.

Explaining to her that George of the Jungle was white didn't stop the woman from seeing what she wanted to see.

We were living on a small acreage at the time and had paid for the property because we wanted our kids to have room to play outside. So mostly what they did was build forts.

Starter forts are usually nothing but a couch cushion propped up in front of the end table. Blankets draped over chairs are added next. My kids built forts in the tall grass. They built forts out of lumber from a house going up in the neighborhood. They built them out of blankets and kitchen chairs.

My experience is no one plays in the forts—they just build them, rearrange them, fight over territory within them; but once the structure has been completed, the kids go play somewhere else.

Personally, I think this is training for being an adult. Adults purchase a starter home, then a bigger and better home; this they repaint and remodel. Once their dream home has been acquired and tastefully furnished, these adults buy an RV and go play somewhere else.

One of the most elaborate forts, and, as it turned out, the most useful fort, constructed at our house was in our unfinished basement.

With youthful exuberance, my older son and two neighbor boys hung rope from the 2 by 4's which would one day frame the basement. There was a spider web of cords strung all through the lower level of our home.

From my perspective, the blankets and sheets dangling over these ropes were randomly hung, but with their superior intelligence the boys knew which flannel walls made up the fort's spacious living room, the office and the play room. The fort also boasted separate bedrooms for the four architects, and then feeling unusually generous, they had added a small room for 2-year-old Colton who had been working feverishly to be part of the construction crew.

After several days of diligent attention, the fort was pronounced completed and I did a home inspection tour. Crawling behind the boys through the unstable walls I oohed and awed over the lovely faux fireplace they had made from a stack of books. I pronounced the old carpet scrap beds lovely. When we got to the small room with the metal bucket, I got claustrophobia so I crawled backward assuming I was leaving the kitchen area and the bucket was a sink for doing dishes.

Since the fort was done, I assumed they'd be off to play somewhere else. I was right. But unlike other forts, these boys were so attached to this structure they visited it randomly throughout the day. They'd be riding their bikes in the driveway and suddenly one of them would slam through the door, barrel down the stairs and spend a few moments behind the blankets. Even Colton would leave his little bike at the end of the walk and run downstairs.

That's when I learned the bucket wasn't a sink at all. And this might not be the most pleasant way to potty train a 2-year-old, but I must say it was the quickest method I've found.

Chapter 7

Just because he could pee in a bucket didn't mean he always did. Surrounding our property and adjoined by the same private road were ten other homes on three-acre lots. The only traffic on our stretch of asphalt was our neighbors. One day Colton was with his best friend, Seth, a very blond, light-skinned child who didn't wait for an invitation to walk in the house and announce his presence. They were standing at the end of the driveway. Both boys wore faded t-shirts and sandals. From where I stood on the porch, their shorts seemed to have disappeared and the contrast between their two bare behinds was noteworthy.

"What are you doing?" I asked the two pantless 3-year-olds.

"We're going to pee on the next car," Colton told me as I approached them.

"Why?" I asked.

The boys looked at one another. That was a question they hadn't considered.

When Colton and Seth were 8, they remained inseparable, although as far as I know they had given up peeing on cars. Still, one day my son mentioned he didn't have any good friends that were black.

"Do you wish Seth was black?" I asked.

"No," Colton said thoughtfully. "I just wish Seth and I had another friend we liked that was black."

When he was still young enough to not have verbalized his desire for a black friend, Colton was going to be a cowboy. His grandfather owned horses, and the young boy liked ropes and swords: two items he often carried around even while riding a stick horse.

If not accurate in melody or words, Colton's song was recognizable. "If you're happy and you know it run your horse. If you're happy and you know it hit your horse."

Unmindful of the preschooler's choice of music, I was helping a woman sort prizes for a PTA raffle we had helped sponsor. We sat around the kitchen table, Joyce Hall, her daughter, who was approximately my age, and myself.

Joyce had been in our home frequently. She hugged my children and they screamed, "Hi, Mrs. Hall," when they saw her in the school parking lot. But she was also of another generation. I could see she was distracted by this distorted version of Colton's song, and I was trying to think of some place to send him on a cold afternoon.

He'd interrupted us earlier, galloping up on the broom. "This is Grandpa's horse, Nickel," Colton explained. "I'm going to ride him fast like this." The horse and rider made a large figure eight out of the dining room through the living room and back to prance in front of us.

"Grandpa will say, 'Colton, you're a good cowboy boy,' when I ride Nickel."

"Your grandpa's horse is named Nickel?" asked Joyce.

"'Cause he ain't worth a dime," Colton said in a gruff imitation of my father.

The little boy pivoted his mount and beating at the straw bristles of the horse head with a plastic sword, the two headed for the bedroom corral.

"He likes horses." the older woman said mildly surprised. "I've never seen a black cowboy."

"Bill Pickett was a former slave and he actually invented bulldogging," I started and then explained how several national champion ropers that year were black. Historically a lot of the original cowboys had been African-American. My voice eventually trailed off. The woman's eyes had glazed over. She wasn't interested in rodeo, and Colton was back. He was amusing himself by swinging a lifeless stuffed horse over the railing and jerking it to safety from an imaginary shark. "If you're happy and you know it feed a shark. If you're happy and you know it feed a shark."

Joyce studied him for a moment and then said thoughtfully, "He really is kind of violent."

What? Because he tied a stuffed animal to a rope? Had she seen computer games lately and all the white kids sitting around choosing between an M16 rifle or an Uzi to shoot realistic looking cops?

Yet, I understood this woman, old enough to be my grandmother. Her visual image of young blacks has been what the media portrayed.

So much of what people say is not meant to be prejudiced nor rude. Simply it is an awareness of the humanness of people who look different from us. We learn and grow by the experiences we have, by the people we know, by the children we love. I feel incredibly blessed to feel so connected to children who look so dissimilar to myself.

Joyce was not the only one hindered by visual images surrounding her. Our little neighbor, Katrina, was too.

I can't marry Isaac," Alexis announced rather sorrowfully one day after school.

I wasn't aware she had planned on marrying Isaac. They played well together, but I had thought the affair was strictly platonic. She had asked only a few days previously if she could marry Jaren. Jaren was tall, good-looking, very nice to 6-year-old girls such as Alexis, and he was getting ready to go to college.

"Jaren can't get married until he graduates," had been my response.

"Okay," she said amiably. As long as the plans were made and she didn't have to worry about who her husband was to be, she was content to wait.

"Why can't you marry, Isaac?" I now asked.

"We don't match," Alexis said sadly.

Isaac was an African-American child in her kindergarten class. He was well-liked and always seemed to be headed to someone's house to play.

"Who said you two didn't match?"

"Katrina, on the bus. Isaac and I were playing and Katrina said you have to match your husband so you will look good in your pictures when you get married."

Katrina was a couple years older than Alexis and was one of eight children. Her parents matched--hair color, complexion--everything similar. Until I got to know the family, telling the children apart was difficult. Stepping stone octuplets, they all matched. To Katrina proper families matched. But how to explain proper families can be diverse not joined by matching complexions or hair coloring, but by love, understanding, experiences and loyalty? I don't think Alexis was concerned about marrying Isaac, but in some unfathomable way she understood how her not being able to marry Isaac put limits on marriage and families. Limits she didn't want.

Actually, when the kids were small, I was seldom offended by the comments, amused sometimes, but fully aware what people said to us is exactly what I would have said 20 years ago before we started our family. Offended we aren't, but surprised at how differently we view the creation of our family from how others view it. We don't mind talking about adoption, but we certainly don't see adoption or race as the first identity of our children. There are so many wonderful and neat facets about them as individuals we would love to bore you with.

Occasionally someone pays us what he feels is a compliment. "I really admire you for taking on kids like those." Taking on kids like ours brought us some incredible experiences-- flickers of understanding impossible to write, and during those flashes of knowledge we've come to believe our children are probably the greater souls who give us more and teach us more than we do them. We are not to be admired for bringing individuals better than ourselves into our home.

My cousin was on a long flight with his recently adopted son. After hearing about the child's ordeal in a foreign orphanage and the subsequent adoption, a man in the next seat said, "That kid just hit the jackpot."

"He didn't understand," stated my cousin. "I'm the lucky one. I'm the one that hit the jackpot being allowed to have this child in my home."

Chapter 8

The idea to adopt a fourth time came slowly. We had three children. They fit the house. They got along. We knew we loved our children and maybe having another black child would be good for Colton. But it wasn't like we were collecting kids or trying to make a statement. But if there was a child who needed a home, we were willing to love a child.

When a friend told us of an agency that had an abundance of children, I thought it was a sign we should try again. Be careful of signs.

I called the agency's director and she answered the phone. In the next year we worked with the agency, I never again got the director on the phone the first try.

Explaining we had a current foster care license and could easily complete a home study, she promised to send her agencies' papers and we hung up.

Three hours later, dinner was on the table, chicken was served, potatoes were buttered. Then Kathy called back.

"We have a 5-month-old baby coming from Florida. You said you'd consider an older baby, and I knew this child must be yours. It has to be. The call came right after yours. This baby sounds perfect. The birth mother is prepared to fly the child here. We've already gotten flight schedules and just need to coordinate with her on when she wants to leave.

"We'll have to make arrangements for interstate compact. She needs to approve you as a family from your bio. Fax it to me first thing in the morning with your home study." She hung up.

I picked at the meal. That fast, we were going to have a new child. We needed to wash clothes, move beds, find a new crib, transfer some money to pay flights, attorney fees and agency fees. But we would soon hold a new baby.

My body's entire focus was on this child. What was he doing right now? Was he being left unattended in a crib because no one wanted him? Was the room drab and hot? Were his clothes clean? Was he doing age-appropriate things or was he lying listless in a dark room without curtains? Did he hear harsh words yelled from his caregivers or did they cry softly because they couldn't keep him? Was he familiar to cuddling and love or was he scared of people because they brought pain?

Would we need clothes? Would he come with some? Should we fly there and require a medical examination? Could we teach him to bond? Would we be so strange to him he wouldn't want to bond?

The kids ate heartily. My husband and I picked at our meal wondering afterward if we ate anything.

I canceled an appointment the next day, scared I'd be gone when the agency called. I rushed to fax our file then went home to wait. Adrenaline needled my fingers every time the phone rang. I got impatient when a neighbor called. I cut short a phone call from my sister and twice made sure the answering machine was working before I left to take our oldest to dance lessons.

No one called that day, nor the next, nor the next. In the next couple weeks, the excitement turned to anger. Finally, I got the agency on the phone.

"Oh," said the director, "that birth mother never did board the plane. I just don't think she was too committed."

What happened to, "I know this is your baby."?

Three weeks before Christmas, Kathy called again. She knew for sure she had our baby. "It's not born yet. The birth mother would like to fly out here to give birth. It would make things easier for her. She needs to be out of the situation she is in at home."

So, of course, we bought the girl a plane ticket and asked her to live with my sister about 300 miles from our home. More diligently than I would follow my own pregnancy, we followed hers. Through my sister, we got the birth mother medical attention and sent Christmas presents to another daughter she had back home. We bought the birth mother suitable clothes for the colder climate and arranged our schedule so we could talk to her on the phone.

We answered her questions as honestly as we could, knowing we were being auditioned for a huge role.

We told the neighbors about the new baby we were getting and pestered them to write letters of recommendation so as to update our home study file. We had law enforcement officials search for our names on court records to prove we were law-abiding citizens. We prayed our fingerprints would come back from the FBI search. We again surrendered our home to inspection and answered personal questions about our marital relationship. We talked about extended family, submitting to a gene-o-gram to understand our family dynamic more accurately.

I had already been attending state-required classes for foster parents and potential adoptive parents. These sessions included classes on dealing with grief, discipline, relationships and special needs of adopted children. I listened to discussions about teaching various cultures to my children and instilling pride within minorities.

Social workers filled out questionnaires about our disciplinary style, our eating habits, and our educational involvement. Then they interviewed the children.

"Do you miss your real mother?" a social worker asked our daughter. "Have you had an opportunity to grieve her rejection of you?"

The questions irritated me for several reasons. First, our 6-year-old daughter didn't understand the concept of real, and, secondly, I had tried hard to explain why my children were placed for adoption. None of their placements were a result of rejection by anyone. These adoptions were because two sets of parents loved them. One set loved her enough to fly in the face of current trends and place her where there were better opportunities. Another set of parents loved her enough to accept her as she is.

When the women started to question our 4-year-old son, I knew she had no understanding of child development.

"Do you wish you understood your culture better?" The poor kid didn't even know what the word culture meant.

"Would you like more information on the culture you would have been exposed to with your biological mother?" Garrett just looked at this woman. He was only a quarter black. His hair, which used to be almost blond in the summer, had started to turn darker but was losing most of the curl.

Garrett has a beautiful birth mother who was barely 15-years-old. She was being raised by a single mother and wanted her son to have a father.

None of the scrutiny was new. We'd been intruded on before, but were always surprised at how the intrusion felt. The first forms we completed for adoption were, of course, the hardest. As I filled out the papers that first time, I kept seeing Joy and Kelly, two of my high school students from a few years back. They were charming girls, beautiful to look at and talented. They were not in my Behavior Disorder classes but in a gifted class, hand-picked to give talented students a head start. I taught both girls as freshmen and then again through part of their sophomore year. Within a couple months of each other, both Joy and Kelly got pregnant and entered the alternative high school program. In their junior year, they would take their babies to the mother's class where they studied, and the babies were cared for. Often after school, Kelly and Joy would walk across the street to the regular high school and visit me in my classroom. They helped me gather books and straighten chairs as they told me about their day, the boring teacher at the alternative place, and what the babies were doing. Typically they would decide they had time to run to a local fast food place and see who was "hanging out."

"Don't you guys have to get your kids?"

"Oh, no. Not for a while. The state pays the babysitter for a couple more hours."

The state paid their babysitters, and I had to beg for a child. I sat there and thought of Joy and Kelly and answered the following:

"What thoughts and feelings do you have which help you believe you can love and be loved by a child born to someone else?"

"What experience or education have you had which will help you transform the birth parents' child into your child?"

"Describe your feelings regarding birth parents."

"Why are you applying for adoption?"

"What is your plan for child care?"

"Describe your methods to teach and discipline your children."

"What plans do you have for savings and retirement?"

"What is your plan for paying the adoption fee?"

"What is the role of religion in your life?"

"Explain your health and life insurance coverage."

This particular questionnaire had over 50 such questions. Exhausting to answer; however, I have since become an advocate of detailed home studies. If my daughter needed to place a child, we would want all the information possible to make a decision as to where that child should go.

This fourth time filling out papers was the most complicated because we had the other children, and they had to answer or attempt to answer questions. However, this time we knew how wonderful bringing a child into our home was, and we were more excited than ever because our children were sharing in the excitement. Alexis told her class at school she was getting a new baby brother. A knowledgeable grade school boy scrutinized me when I went in to help as a reading mother.

"I don't think you're getting no brother too soon," he remarked.

"Am too," Alexis insisted.

The boy shook his head disgusted but not sure enough of the facts of life to explain them to someone so ignorant. Moms had to get fatter than me to get new babies.

Three o'clock Christmas Eve morning the phone rang. Without turning on a light I grabbed the receiver on the second ring.

"I just took her to the hospital," my sister said. "Baby should be here anytime."

For three hours I lay in the dark watching the clock numbers slowly flip. I wondered what was happening in a brightly lit maternity room hundreds of miles away. Had the baby cried yet? Was the birth mother in too much pain?

At six o'clock, I finally got up to move around the quiet house. I mopped the floor and rearranged the decorations on the Christmas tree. Dry pine needles fell on the wrapped packages below. I brought baby clothes up from the basement and washed them in a mild cycle using a vinegar rinse in case the baby was prone to skin rash.

Tense and willing the phone to ring again, the sound still startled me.

"He's so cute," Donna gushed. "He's adorable. Linda wouldn't hold him. She doesn't want to grow attached to him. He was born at 6:40 a.m."

All states have different relinquishment laws, but generally no birthmother can sign consent for adoption sooner than twenty-four hours after she has returned from recovery.

"Is Kathy willing to interrupt her family's Christmas morning to drive to the hospital for relinquishment?"

"Kathy will have to come Christmas morning," my sister said as excited about this baby as we were. "Linda wants to hand the baby right to you guys."

"Will it be early morning or later. Should we drive down tonight, or early in the morning?

"You'd probably better come tonight. I'll call you."

Excitedly we made plans. My parents had time to come for a midafternoon Christmas dinner. We told the kids their new baby brother had been born. Garrett, then 4, was immensely impressed, and rushed out to tell the neighbors about the new "little guy." Garrett then spent the rest of the morning digging in the toy box trying to find the perfect gift to give the new addition.

Carefully, I selected clothes for the children to wear. Carefully, I selected clothing for my husband and me. Carefully, I folded them into suitcases so they wouldn't wrinkle. I wanted the birth mother to have no concerns about the kind of family she was placing this child with.

My parents brought a new dresser and helped us set up the crib. We packed newborn clothes and wondered if we should go get diapers now or enroute. Food was part of the Christmas tradition and so we ate sweet potatoes and pie and urged the clock toward a phone call. The kids opened all the presents under the tree and my parents helped us clear away ribbon and torn wrapping paper so the house would be inviting for the new arrival.

Crossing state lines with a new baby requires getting permission from judges in both states. We knew this could take at least a week or maybe longer during the holiday season, so we took down our Christmas tree and cleaned everything perishable out of the fridge, pushing it on to neighbors who already had overstocked holiday refrigerators.

After completing our Christmas celebrating and cleanup, we could no longer stand the uncertainty of when we were to hold our new child. So we called.

"I'll call you back. Linda is not sure that she wants to place on Christmas day. It might ruin Christmas for her from now on; probably first thing on the 26th, she's thinking. I'll call you," Kathy said.

"When?"

"Uh, soon?"

My sister called after and wondered if we could all eat Christmas dinner together.

"You need to come and we'll all have Christmas dinner together, you and Linda and the new baby. That's what she wants."

"So she can look us over?"

"Well, she wants to be sure."

"When are we leaving," Garrett kept asking. "When are we going?"

"Early tomorrow morning," we told the children.

So rather than leave Christmas Eve, we told the kids we'd leave early in the morning. Right after they saw what Santa left them.

"We'll get my brother tomorrow?" Garrett asked no one in particular. "We'll get him tomorrow," and then padded off to bed.

In our excitement to leave Christmas Eve, my husband and I had decided we'd load the kids in the car and then run back in and place the bikes each of them were getting by the Christmas stockings. That way when we got back in several days, the three children would have another Christmas. Now we weren't leaving until in the morning; the kids would wake up to nothing but bikes.

Children all over the world were waking up to much less than an expensive bike. My children had already received more presents than they needed. But a melancholy settled over me as we put each of them to bed and Kathy hadn't yet phoned.

"There's nothing to put in their socks," I told Clare as if it were his fault. "Just those stupid penny collection books you wanted so you pretended the kids should have them. My kids ought to have better than that for Christmas morning." I left the house about 10:30 Christmas Eve to get stocking stuffers.

The windshield wipers slapped hard at the fluffy snow and I growled at the perfect Christmas Eve night. Even 24-hour grocery stores have the sense to close on Christmas Eve. Their closure was a place to project my displaced anger. Anger at having no control over when and how we got our children. Anger that we had to dance through so many hoops to get a baby. Anger that we sat and waited in such an undignified manner for someone to call so we could run like silly puppies.

Seven-Eleven stores haven't much in the way of stocking stuffers.

Buying lifesavers and pop as Christmas morning surprises probably would have thrilled my children, but would have made things seem even less like Christmas than our treeless living room. I cried and drove to the truck stop ten miles out of town. The gift shop had necklaces and mugs so overpriced no child should be allowed to touch them much less own them. The cashier rang up my purchases just as the radio wished us a Merry Christmas. It was midnight.

Kathy had called while I was out. The social worker had spent much of the afternoon with the birth mother and they all thought it would be good for her emotional stability if the baby wasn't placed until after Christmas, but the birth mother would be released from the hospital Christmas morning and would like to eat Christmas dinner with us that afternoon. "Get to know you and your children."

Clare and I were concerned. This was an audition.

The kids were excited about the bikes, thought the necklaces and mugs were okay, but were fascinated with those penny collections. The snow was still falling as we loaded suitcases. The car wouldn't have enough seatbelts to bring the baby home so we were taking the pickup with an extended cab. Each suitcase had to be covered with a water proof tarp and we were trying to hurry. We promised the kids breakfast at a restaurant since there was no milk in the fridge, having given it to a semi-grateful neighbor. Excited children waited in the truck as I rushed into the house for one last-minute item. The light on the answering machine was blinking. "I'm not calling anyone back," I thought but pushed the button out of curiosity.

"I hope you haven't left yet," Kathy's voice was unmistakable, "Linda has changed her mind. She's decided not to place."

We physically forced Garrett back into the house. He sat in the corner of the couch, his head on his folded arms, and sobbed. "I wanted to see my little brother. I wanted to see my little brother."

I had to go back out to the truck stop for an over-priced quart of milk so we could eat breakfast.

Linda flew home with her baby using the round trip ticket we'd bought her nearly a month earlier.

Alexis had to deal with being called a liar at school. I had to repack the clean baby clothes and put away the crib.

In January, another child fell through. The agency sent us a $1,500 bill, a processing fee for helping us find a baby.

Chapter 9

"Why?" is a question we are often asked. Our answers are often foolish, sometimes flippant. If the questioner seems sincere, we try hard to be honest, but always our answers are incomplete. There is no way we can adequately describe the experiences which led us to adopt again. Regardless of our hesitancy to discuss why, we want it understood how we were always comforted with knowledge our home should welcome each child.

About 9:30 on a typical Sunday evening we got a phone call. A baby had been born that morning, full black mother, unknown father, supposedly no drugs, seems healthy.

"More than ten thousand dollars in bills come with this child plus attorney fees, interstate compact fees, agency compensation, and some cost of living expenses for the birth mother, but he's cute. Do you want him? He really needs a home."

"Has relinquishment been signed?"

"Tomorrow morning. She's really going to sign."

"I've heard that before. Has she been AIDS tested?"

"Oh, I'm sure. That's standard procedure."

"How much more than ten thousand dollars?"

"I'm not sure. We'll have to wait until all the bills come in."

"Weight, height?"

"I don't know. You'll have to check in the morning. Why don't you guys come tonight and then you can have him first thing in the morning?"

"We can't just wake the kids up and drive all night. We have to decide first."

"Take your time, but you don't want him shuttled to foster care. That makes things complicated. You should have him right away."

Clare and I talked about money. We talked about the unknowns of this child. We talked about feelings we'd had for nearly a year. But mostly we talked about how I was now six months pregnant. If I finally carried a baby full term and we adopted this little boy, we would have two infants. Could we deal with a newborn while I was in the final stages of pregnancy? What if my doctor's worse-case scenario occurred and I was in bed for a while? Where would we get the money for this child, a new car to fit five children, and money to pay our percentage of our rather inadequate maternity insurance? Where would we get the patience to deal with five? Would we have enough wisdom to raise these kids? Where would we get another crib, enough diapers, and formula? Would anyone ever let us visit them again? How would I ever find five matching pairs of socks on Sunday mornings when church started at nine?

This child and the one I was carrying would give us five children under seven. Five children is a whole lot more than the measly four children we had been prepared to handle just last Christmas.

Clare listened to my concerns and even sympathized with my unvoiced ones then went for a walk. He was kind but emphatic about his need to get away from my constant babble.

After a long stroll in the comforting dark, Clare made his decision. He was sleeping peacefully by midnight. I stewed until twilight and then slept through the alarm.

Not until we heard the birthmother had signed relinquishment did I call my parents. Their excitement over our new son was contagious. When I tried to throw a damper on it by suggesting we "might be getting ourselves in pretty deep," my mother wouldn't even listen. "If you need help, we'll just bring some of those babies here."

The drive to get our first child had seemed endless. "Someone cut the end off this road," I had thought six years earlier when we had gone to pick up Alexis. We'd packed quickly and traveled light like childless people do. Even now as I type, the excitement of going makes my fingers tremble. She was my little girl from the second they laid her in my arms. She looked up at me and then opened her mouth. I thought she was going to cry. I didn't know what to do if she did. If I couldn't stop her from crying, would they let her stay with us?

Each trip gets more exciting because now the excitement is compounded with the anticipation and enthusiasm of the other children. On this trip to get William, Alexis' stomach tickled, and her heart hurt from anticipation. We had to stop so she could throw up - something she often did when overly excited. We had thought we were excited to go and get our first child. This trip had the three older ones bouncing. I was kept grounded with a late case of morning sickness and a backache.

We held a tiny newborn. The kids poked at him. They pulled off his socks to look at his toes. They rubbed his black curls and marveled at his tiny brown ears. No visual evidence suggested he was meant to be in our home. I'd come a long ways. Because, except for figuring out how to get all those socks on before church and where we'd find the patience and wisdom, there was no hesitation. We didn't doubt he was meant to be with us.

Just before Keeley was to be born I thought it was time to see if we couldn't teach William to sleep the night. On a couple nights when Clare was gone, I tried to let the newborn cry. His fussing woke up his unborn sister. She would toss and roll and agitate over her brother's displeasure. She remains the same way to this day. Until they were well into their third year, regardless of which room William was in, if he woke up, she did, too.

The neighbors showered us with help. Thoughtful, appropriate help. A couple women asked if I'd like a shower. I begged no. I didn't want people feeling obligated to buy things and come. I just didn't want to be the center of help. A neighbor and friend didn't ask permission but gave me a "dinner" open house. They served pizza and invited people to bring frozen meals for us. Food flowed in. One lady brought a cake rather than the assigned main dish. She set it smartly on the counter and announced, "Man does not live by casseroles alone." Another woman brought all the fixings for a picnic lunch: hot dogs, chips, pork and beans, individual juices, cupcakes. We were so overwhelmed. I didn't cook for nearly a month after Keeley was born.

The older kids never seemed jealous. They didn't even complain when a baby was sleeping where one of the older ones typically came for a morning snuggle. We had often read in bed or watched the news. This ritual was somewhat curtailed by the onslaught of babies.

One morning I was feeding a baby in the rocking chair when Garrett came shivering into the bedroom.

"Honey," I said, "why don't you crawl under my covers and get warm."

The 5-year-old bounded onto the bedspread and then pointed at the blankets. Seriously and without a hint of ire he asked, "Is there any pee in there?"

"No."

"Is there any throw up in there?"

"Not this morning," I told him.

Delighted he crawled under the quilts. My children learn fast and adapt well.

Keri was in middle school and we were fortunate enough to have her living next door. She showered our children with attention and they would watch for the school bus hoping their friend would come over. One evening, we left her with the three older children while Clare and I took William and Keeley to the grocery store.

The weather was chilly and the two infants were bundled tightly. A blanket had been thrown over each of their faces to ward off the night breeze. Both baby carriers fit side-by-side in the grocery cart.

"Oh, twins," one lady said excitedly as she lined up behind us in the checkout aisle.

Clare said nothing. He paid for the groceries and reached to pick up our bags.

"I bet it is so much fun having little twins," the lady trilled and then reached over, first removing one blanket and then the other blanket revealing William's brown face and then Keeley's pale complexion.

"The egg split," Clare said, nodding to the two infants still blinking into the lights.

The woman's face was a study in confusion, "Egg split?" We could almost see her thoughts. "That would produce identical twins. They don't seem identical."

As the babies grew, our older three took great pride in every accomplishment.

"Grandpa, Willy rolled over today," Garrett bragged over the phone. "And I only had to push him a little."

"We're practicing for show and tell," Alexis explained as she balanced her 6-month-old sister in the middle of the living room. "I want Keeley to be able to sit right when I take her to class."

Neighborhood friends often had to endure lengthy descriptions of the babies' new accomplishments.

"Did you see how Keeley can walk now?" Garrett asked a friend.

The little girl was balancing herself against the couch, inching her way along the edge. Garrett applauded her efforts and told her she was a good walker. She grinned excitedly, lost her balance, and toppled onto one side. Looking up, she squealed happily at her brother and hero.

Garrett's friend glanced at the baby, "Can we go now? I hate to see snot."

At first Alexis enjoyed telling her friends that both of the babies were in her family. She carefully recounted how one was in my stomach and we had to go get the other one.

"Then he's not your brother."

"He is," Alexis would say forcefully and a little defensively.

Chapter 10

Moving to new schools, new neighborhoods and new churches is always fraught with the traditional settling in problems, but our family has additional issues. Hopefully, we handle them with good humor, but some of our humor wouldn't be understood so we keep it to ourselves. Like when a new neighbor brought over fudge as a housewarming gift. She stared for several moments and then asked, "Are any of these your real children?"

"Oh, none of these are real," I wanted to say. "We keep the real ones in a safe place so they won't get worn out or stolen."

When the subject of "real" comes up, my husband often wants to tell people life would be easier if they weren't real. "They all run on Duracell. We disconnect the batteries so at night we can rest."

Missy was a 5-year-old in one of William's play groups. She obviously loved lace and fancy hair ribbons. But the bows couldn't hide the fact that her hair was fine and straight, defying her mother's heroic efforts with the curling iron. She was a white blond from traditional European stock and William's hair fascinated her. He'd given up trying to get her to leave him alone. As often as he pulled away and hid behind me, the fancy little lady crept closer and rubbed his head. Finally, she looked up at me and demanded, "Why don't you comb his tangles out?"

One good church lady, sensitive to the word "real," always introduced Keeley as our natural-born child. If Keeley's birth was natural, how come it required so many strangers posing as medical experts and so many needles squirting synthetic compounds? Yet, if Keeley is our "natural" child that makes the others what--unnatural?

Once I was listening as my daughter played Barbies with two neighbor girls. One of the girls, Alisa, refused to be the black Barbie.

"That would be gross," she said "being black." She picked up the black doll and tossed it behind the couch.

My first inclination was to chuck Alisa through the window behind the couch. I felt sick that someone would feel being black was gross. I was so angry.

"Most blacks would find being like you gross," I wanted to tell the girl. "In fact most people would be grossed out being like you."

I wanted to shake my own daughter for not saying something in support of the blackness of her brothers. But how could I expect my daughter to say something profound when, to this day, I don't know the proper way to have handled that situation? My gut impulse was to throw the speaker out of my house and tell her never to come back until she could leave her prejudices home. I wanted her to figure out that God loved all of his children, not just the pasty white, little, anemic ones.

"You ever heard about unconditional love?" I wanted to ask her. "You ever heard that God made us all and loves us all?" Finally the obvious became obvious. I certainly wasn't displaying anything akin to unconditional love for my daughter's friend.

I abruptly realized that if I didn't allow Alisa in my home she would probably never get to know races that were different from her own. Maybe being here would change her and help her.

Prior to getting our children, a man we knew from church told us about a break he made with a good friend.

"We knew each other in high school," this man told me. "We went fishing together and out to dinner. A couple years after my wife and I adopted our two little girls from India my friend admitted to me that he could hardly stand to look at my girls, that he found no beauty in them. I've refused to have anything to do with him since."

When the little Barbie doll-playing girl refused to be black, I understood the emotion which ended a lifelong friendship. However, somehow I've decided there must be a happy medium. If I refuse to associate with those who disagree with how I adore my children, then I rob those people of the chance to understand why I adore my children.

We tried to hold to this standard as the kids have gotten older; however, there is a limit to what we will allow. Some words and some attitudes will not be tolerated. Our children do not have to be subjected to prejudicial treatment in their own home. Don't come to my home and display bias.

That afternoon I didn't handle the situation correctly, but something in me just wouldn't let them work it out alone. I dug the dark doll out from behind the couch and sat down amongst the girls.

"Which doll do you like best?" I nonchalantly asked holding the three Barbies.

"I like this one," said the girl whose hair I still felt like ripping out. Alisa tried to pull the doll from my hand and claim ownership of the long white-haired figure. I held firmly onto the dolls and pretended to study them intently.

"Which one do you like best?" I asked my daughter. She hesitated. Finally she pointed vaguely to a white doll with light brown hair. "Why?" I asked, my irritation starting to show. She hesitated again and then shrugged.

"I don't like either one of these dolls," I said, motioning to the two favored Barbies. "They look like they never go outside. Like all they do is sit inside and watch TV. Pretty boring."

My daughter tensed. Refusing to look at her, I kept studying the dolls. "Maybe it's time you guys all went out and played something else or you'll start looking pale and unhealthy like these dolls."

Tears trickled slowly down Alexis' face. Angrily she tried to stop any evidence of her crying. She rushed out just as the phone rang. Alisa and her friend left and I tried to hurry through a phone call. When I finally found Alexis, she was sitting on the side of her brothers' bunk bed.

"You hate me," she said fiercely. "You hate my color. I'm peach just like that doll."

I didn't say anything. Not because I'm particularly patient or content to use the wise silent approach, I didn't know what to say.

"You like the boys better. You hate me. You think people that look peach color are ugly." She cried. And I let her. I could have pointed out that I, too, was peach, a rather older, rounder, more wrinkled version of peach, but peach nonetheless. I held her, but I still didn't say anything. My little baby, grown so she hardly fit on my lap, sobbed into my shoulder as she clarified why I hated her.

"That doll looks just like me," she cried.

Now was not the time to explain that short of surgery or mutation no living woman looked like a Barbie.

"Her hair is like mine."

"Except proportionally it's three feet longer," I thought.

"Her eyes are blue just like mine."

"With eyeliner and twenty-one coats of mascara your eyes would look similar," I agreed silently.

"She's wearing clothes just like mine."

The Barbie had a spandex workout suit on similar to the outfit Alexis had used for an acrobat recital. Of course, the Barbie's outfit was tighter, brighter, more revealing, and cost more.

"You hate the way I look, uh?" said Alexis, wiping her nose on my shoulder before looking up at me.

"How does it feel?" I asked, "To think someone hates you because of the way you look?" Maybe she was too young for this discussion but again maybe not.

"Not good."

"Did Colton see Alisa throw that doll?"

"I don't know."

"How do you think he would feel if he thought you would hate to look like him?"

"Bad."

"I felt bad when no one would play with the black Barbie. It made me feel like maybe no one would want to play with people who are black."

Alexis' surprise was genuine. "I play with Colton." And she did. The two had a unique bond. They shared a belief life should be lived loudly, quickly, immediately. This compatible spirit often erupted into noisy games, teasing and loud denials of responsibility for whatever was broken, missing or leaking onto the carpet. In psychological jargon they "egged each other on." This was the reason they didn't sit by each other at the dinner table or in the car. They wanted to; we purposely kept them separated.

Alexis and I talked for a long time, interrupted only every ninety seconds by boys who needed their remote control car, a pillow, clean socks (like they ever changed their socks), and a host of other excuses to see what we were doing.

"Mom," Alexis finally said. "I just like that doll best because she's got holes in her ears." Alexis was fascinated by pierced ears. I told her she could have hers pierced when she'd learned to play three songs on the piano. So far she was wearing clip ons.

"I like your color," I told her as we left the room.

"I like Colton's and William's color," she told me.

Chapter 11

Several times, Alexis has asked, “Do you remember when I thought you didn’t like peach people?” Since that day she has been more vocal in her support of anyone she perceives is being unjustly maligned.

Garrett is a practical kind of kid that is oblivious to a lot of mundane life issues. He can eat mashed potatoes hot or cold. Clothes should be big so as not to hinder movement. As a kid he saved neat looking pictures, broken darts and dead batteries. He bossed his brothers around, defended them in front of others, and expected obedience from them at home.

One day he was staring at his brother’s head. “I’m sure glad I don’t have hair like Colton’s,” he announced.

“And why not?” I demanded, vigilant in my desire that the children display loyalty to one another. “What’s wrong with his hair?”

“It probably still has glass in it,” said Garrett conclusively.

I grinned. Over a month earlier the two boys had opened the living room window to let in some winter air. “We’re so hot,” they explained when I told them to close it. The two had been wrestling and they looked hot. For several seconds the boys ignored me and enjoyed the arctic air. "Close it," I insisted as the furnace kicked on.

The windows were state of the art, top of the line argon, gas-filled, thermal panes that swung down to facilitate easy cleaning. Somehow the boys put so much uneven pressure on the window, it pulled out and hit Colton on the head. Glass shattered into tiny slivers. Splinters were in the couch, across the carpet, and embedded in Colton's head. For one split second, I could see the glass shining in the black curls. The next minute there was red blood percolating up through the curls and drenching his head. Red dripped down his forehead and spilled over his ears.

Outside, Clare heard the crash and from past experience knew something would need to be fixed. He wasn't prepared for the intensity of our crisis. We didn't know what to do. We didn't know if there was glass sticking into the little boy's head or just caught in his hair. We rushed the screaming child to the sink and ran water over his head. Probably not the Red Cross recommended procedure to promote clotting and curtail bleeding.

Glass fell onto the porcelain now turning red from the blood. I forcibly held the little boy's head while Clare carefully dug through the curls and tried to find any more glass. A nurse from across the street came. She called a physician and asked for advice. Meanwhile, Clare and I used the vacuum hose to try to suck the glass out, another method not recommended by the Red Cross to control bleeding. We tried combing through the matted curls. The doctor's best suggestion was a power sprayer. We drenched the complaining child while Garrett sat out on the front porch shivering and berating himself for causing the probable death of his brother.

Eventually we shaved Colton's head. Not an easy task considering the head kept moving, the hair was thick and wet, and glass chips dulled the blades. We found no big gashes, only dozens of superficial cuts which bled with incredible vitality.

Considering Garrett's experience with his brother and the likelihood of more accidents, I understood his position concerning hair type. That night we decided even if Colton's hair did look good, those good looks came with a down side.

Chapter 12

Late one night, I took Alexis and Colton to the grocery store. The day before we had bought them backpacks because school was going to start in a few days. Colton would enter kindergarten, Garrett would be in second grade, Alexis in fourth.

The two weren't exactly well-behaved as I shopped for food. They teased each other. They sang songs in the cart. We stood in line and they growled deep in their throats like angry dogs and then peeled with laughter when other late night shoppers looked their way. They refused to bag the groceries correctly. Stacking cabbage on bread and then seeing how high they could get the produce before it toppled to the floor. I tried to ignore them. They weren't doing anything wrong, just irritating. We were headed home by 10:30, and I still had dinner dishes to do as well as put away smashed bread.

The car was dark and I couldn't see my little boy's face. "What do you think is going to be the best thing at kindergarten?" I asked cheerfully, trying to encourage him to be excited about school.

"I think they'll laugh at me." Colton had said similar things so many times. He wouldn't go places with what he calls "strangers." He's not shy; he just doesn't like "strangers." He wouldn't wrestle at one of Garrett's matches where they offered a mat to younger kids. His explanation was, "They are all strangers."

"They're strangers to Garrett, too," I told him. Didn't matter. Colton wouldn't wrestle, and he wouldn't go stand by the school bus when Alexis was getting home from a field trip. We wanted him to direct her and a friend to our car.

"They're strangers," he explained. "I don't know those bus drivers."

I had my suspicions as to what this stranger business was about, but I didn't want to voice my suspicions and by so doing plant an idea in his head. Besides, I didn't want to think I may be right. That night in the car he left no doubt.

"Colton, why would anyone laugh at you?"

"Because," he explained to me as if I were slow, "most of the kids at school are white, and I'm black."

I felt sick. Does he feel so black? Does he make all his decisions of movement among people on the fact he is black? We talked. He was just matter of fact.

"Has anyone ever laughed because you are black?"

"Some of my friends."

"Who, Colton?" I asked, gripping the steering wheel as I waited for a name.

"Long ago, when maybe I was four, or three, or two. He said a bad word and flipped his finger at me."

There was silence, Alexis chattered about being scared, and how Colton was funny and how no one laughed at Isaac, a black student in her grade.

"It gets tiring being the only black person," he said.

I tried to tell him no one was going to laugh in kindergarten, but then I had to be honest. Someday someone will laugh, or be rude, but Colton, only because they are stupid and mean and don't understand. I cried that night. Clare didn't cry like I did, he just wished somehow our children could live without bias.

He wondered again, for the five thousandth time, if we have done right by putting these kids in a no man's land. They're not in a black culture, they're not white.

School actually was good for Colton. He found out people would laugh at him, but mostly because he is funny. Incredibly funny.

Alexis is white and a member of the majority, yet she was raised with black brothers. This was just normal to her. Typical and common. She doesn't understand life any other way. Certainly, most American students received the Weekly Readers featuring Martin Luther King on his birthday. One particular issue explained how black children were not allowed to ride the same school bus as white students. The pictures showed two school buses, one carrying white children, one carrying black.

"That's stupid," my daughter said as she shoved the picture into my face, "to have two school buses. Don't you think that's stupid?"

I just barely had time to agree before she changed her mind. "But maybe it's good, too. If I missed my bus, I could sneak onto the boys' bus and you wouldn't have to drive me to school."

The fact the boys wouldn't have been her brothers totally eluded her.

Chapter 13

School bus rides were frequently the impetus for intolerant teasing and sometimes over-the-top bigoted remarks.

"He called me a Cocoa Puff," Colton huffed one day as he came in from the bus.

"'Cause of your hair?" his sister informed him as she followed him into the living room.

"I know why," Colton hissed.

"Don't listen to him," the older girl said. "He's stupid."

"What if he called you Cocoa Puff?" Colton asked angrily.

"Then he would really be stupid, cause my hair isn't like a Cocoa Puff," she responded mildly.

"You're stupid," he informed her.

"Call him Shredded Wheat," I suggested.

Both kids looked at me startled. I didn't normally advocate name-calling.

"Yeah," Colton laughed. "He's Shredded Wheat. He is. His head is just like Shredded Wheat."

"Well, not exactly like Shredded Wheat," Alexis mused.

"My head's not exactly like Cocoa Puff," Colton retorted.

Within a week, elementary school bus riders were insulting one another with harsher and harsher versions of breakfast cereals.

"You're a Cocoa Puff!"

"You're a Shredded Wheat!"

"Well, you're a Fruit Loop!"

"You're a stupid Cheerio!"

"You're a soggy Frosted Flake!"

The connection between hair and cereal was lost as the youth rattled to school on the big yellow bus while hurling insults at one another.

"You look like soggy oatmeal."

"You smell like burnt toast."

"You smell like a rotten egg."

Okay, so everyone didn't understand the game involved cereal and not other breakfast foods.

Just because we dodged the dry cereal bullet didn't mean there wasn't always another one.

"Seth said some people think black people are stupid," Colton told me one Friday after school.

"Some people do," I told him.

"I got two hundred percent on my reading goal," Colton retorted. "Most people didn't even get 100 percent."

"I know," I said. "You're a good reader."

"And fast," he added. He thought for several minutes and then said, "I'm not stupid."

He's not either. Sometimes, however, he performed as if he was stupid. For a few years he had the best teachers who "got" his sense of humor. Starting in kindergarten, school was a positive experience. Even when we moved to a much more metropolitan area with more diversity, he was fortunate to have excellent teachers. Eventually, our lucky run was destined to end. Colton didn't like his fifth-grade teacher. And the feeling was mutual.

She hated how he wrote reminders with black marker on his hand rather than in the "planner" assigned each student. She disliked his ability to hear the tardy bell, sprint from the classroom door and slide into his seat before the ringing stopped. His sloppy penmanship was irritating, and he never showed his work. His fear of strangers wasn't evident since he knew everyone in the school and he loudly greeted friends across the classroom, playground and cafeteria.

Early in the school year I received notification from the fifth-grade teacher about Colton's upcoming punishment. Exactly what crime he committed, I'm not able to recall, but for restitution, he was required to pick up garbage during lunch.

I signed the note saying this was appropriate. The next day I received a phone call.

"Colton is throwing the garbage into the trashcan like he is playing basketball," the teacher greeted me. "His friends are hauling around the can and applauding when he scores."

"Okay?" I said. "And does he miss and get garbage on the ground or something?"

"That's not the point," the teacher snarled. "He's having fun."

"Oh," I thought. "So the crime here is he's having fun."

"Those other students aren't supposed to be helping."

"Yeah," I thought. "We don't want kids helping each other. That would be bad."

"And then they started wrestling on the grass," she continued listing the sins of her students. "And now they have grass on their clothes."

"Grass isn't good," I thought.

"And Colton keeps scratching," she grumbled.

"As long as he only scratches himself," I wanted to say, but didn't. This woman was not having a good day.

"I don't think picking up garbage is an effective deterrent for Colton," the woman continued.

Actually, the punishment did make an impression on him. He came charging in the house after school and raced to the shower.

"That was so itchy," he said later as he absently scratched himself in vague remembrance of grass. "I'm not wrestling there anymore."

"What about picking up garbage?" I asked.

"Oh, that was fun," he said cheerfully.

His teacher wasn't cheerful during our first scheduled parent/teacher conference.

"I'm doing the best I can with him," she told me testily. "I just don't think he can quite keep up."

"Do you have his last year's standardized scores?" I asked her.

"They are in his file," she spoke wearily, shuffling a couple assignments Colton had completed during the first few weeks of school. The papers were marked heavily with red ink in such a way as to suggest Colton was indeed missing significant chunks of required information.

"Can we see how he compares based on his scores?" I asked.

"We don't compare students," she said, totally unaware of how ironic her statement was. Isn't the whole point of standardized testing to compare growth among schools, states and students?

She also listed other reasons for not wanting to get his file. There wasn't time before the next parents came in. The cabinet where these records were kept was clear on the other side of the room. I was quickly siding with Colton on my feelings for this particular educator.

While we're on the subject of educators we have to discuss Mrs. Rose. Colton was fortunate enough to be dropped in her class on her last year of teaching. This is a year where some teachers are checking out, coasting to the finish. Mrs. Rose was sprinting. She raised money for a 200-mile train ride to visit the glass museum in Tacoma. She published a cookbook of students' favorite recipes. She continued to haul visuals and multiple learning ideas into her classroom.

As a consequence of his earliest skin problems and other struggles, Colton suffered from incredibly poor fine motor skills. Mrs. Rose had some assignments which required considerable writing, an act which Colton hated. This teacher of tweens told him he could commit to memory rather than write. She had recognized his ability to memorize. He memorized all the presidents of the United States. She applauded him and told him his feat was so amazing he needed to go tell this impressive list to the principal. Forewarned, I'm sure, the principal appropriately appreciated this accomplishment and sent Colton to get a free bag of popcorn on popcorn Friday. With popcorn in tow, the fourth-grader waltzed back to class.

"Now you need to memorize all the countries in Africa," Mrs. Rose told him. He did and then all the ones in Europe and South America.

Mrs. Rose saw potential in students; the fifth-grade teacher did not, or at least not in Colton. The overwhelmed fifth-grade teacher was reticent about even walking across the room and retrieving the boy's file. When finally persuaded upon, she sat back at her desk, flipped the folder open, found the appropriate page and then said, "This can't be right."

The scores were higher than she had anticipated. I knew exactly what the scores were. I wanted her to start treating him like he was capable.

Alexis was in the same school system where Colton was enjoying his punishment as a garbage man. His older sister had her own set of detractors. Her first intentional act of stupidity was to superglue her hands together. This was not an accident. This was a conscious choice.

She was in seventh grade which explains a lot. Because, quite frankly, cognizant thinking and middle school kids aren't really a compatible concept. If you've spent as much as an afternoon with sixth and seventh-grade students you know they do things like superglue their palms and fingers together. This is one of their more rational behaviors.

The recess lady phoned me early on a Wednesday afternoon about how my daughter's hands were stuck in a position reminiscent of a humble prayer.

The recess lady is a permanent fixture on the playground. She yells if someone throws a football on the roof. She yells if someone throws a shoe on the roof. She yells if someone throws a small fifth grader on the roof.

With more hostility than concern, the recess lady informed me they would need my permission to take my daughter to the emergency room.

"Because her hands are glued together," I asked, "she needs to go to the emergency room?"

"We know of no other solution."

"May I, please, speak to her?" I requested.

"She can't hold the phone," recess lady said in a tone which suggested Alexis' lack of common sense was due to the kind of parenting the girl had received. "We've sent her to lunch with the rest of her class."

"Can she eat?" I asked

"I assume someone will feed her," the recess lady's attitude indicated she would just as soon see my daughter starve.

I declined the school's gracious offer of medical intervention and recommended we allow Alexis the opportunity to deal with the consequences of mishandling strong adhesives. Which is just as well. Within an hour, the novelty of being an idiot wore off, and she pulled her hands apart.

"They bled a little bit," she told me later and then explained how Paul had come to school with a tube of glue. "We glued our finger and thumb together. Then decided to do my whole hand. I put my hand out. He poured the glue on. I put my hands together. We blew on them for like ten seconds. Then they were stuck."

"Why did you want your hands stuck together?" I asked.

"Peer pressure," she said firmly. "That's what the recess lady said. I am a slave to peer pressure."

"Did he pressure you?" I asked

"No," she scorned. "I wasn't being pressured." She looked at where the skin had pulled off her palm. "I was just acting stupid."

Alexis typified all the stereotypes of a privileged white girl. She's blonde, blue-eyed, skinny and socially acceptable. When she did something stupid, the staff expressed surprise. When Colton did something stupid, there was no surprise. When he scored in the top 90 percentile in vocabulary, at least one educator said, "This can't be right."

From my experience as their mother, they are both equally capable of lapses in judgment as well as shining moments.

As humans, we don't always see things rationally. For several years I wrote a newspaper column about incidents in our home. One day I was struggling to find a topic when Colton came in.

"Sometimes you write about dumb things that we've done," my son said as he watched me type. "Why do you do that?" asked the boy who was only about ten at the time.

"Because I don't know about the dumb things your friends do," I suggested.

"Bryan drowned his guinea pig," my son saidm leaning comfortably on the corner of my desk. "Is that dumb?"

"How did he do that?" I asked.

"Teaching it to swim."

"Yeah, that's dumb," I said, unconcerned.

"His mom was super mad," Colton continued.

"Really?" I asked, still watching the computer screen. "I thought she hated all of Bryan's pets."

"Well, he put it in the freezer and because it was wet from being drowned, the hair stuck to the ice cream carton." Colton explained as he tested my office stapler by stapling the air. The bent wires dropped on the carpet.

"Why did he put it in the freezer?" I asked, taking the stapler from him.

"Cause we were skateboarding and didn't have time for a funeral." Colton picked up a pair of scissors and started clipping the edges of a discarded newspaper. "Bryan thought the pig might start smelling dead."

"So you were there when the guinea pig drowned?" I asked, taking the scissors from him and giving him my full attention. "You guys drowned a little pet?"

"I didn't let him drown," Colton said defensively. "When I looked at him he was zooming around the edge of the wading pool swimming like a dog." Colton raised both hands and mimicked a fast-paced dog paddle. "But then I guess he stopped." Colton stopped paddling with his own hands. "And then he sunk."

My son shook his head sorrowfully. "When we came back, he was at the bottom."

"Colton," I said, "that was irresponsible."

"Bryan's just that way," Colton said as if he were discussing a subordinate. "He's not responsible enough to have a pet."

"Neither are you," I admonished.

"We didn't think he would drown," Colton said defensively.

"What did you think he would do when he got tired of swimming?" I asked. "Roll over on his back and float?"

"Can they do that?" Colton asked.

"Apparently not," I said, dismayed at his lack of foresight and sensitivity.

"Well, I never drowned any of my pets," Colton said in his defense.

"But you helped your friend drown his," I said accusingly.

"You didn't even care about the pig when you thought Bryan did a dumb thing," Colton pointed out, "but now you get all freaked out if I was dumb. The reason you don't write about the dumb things other kids do is because you only notice the dumb things we do."

Mothers, as well as society, tend to notice certain behaviors over others. Certainly I wish protests wouldn't become violent or looting wouldn't occur after certain verdicts. These incidents are more than regrettable. However, do you, or the media for that matter, notice the dumb things sports fans do, including riots after losses or even after wins? Remember the Stanley Cup finals in 2011? Close to 150 people were injured and almost 100 arrested. Cars were lit on fire, buildings damaged, stores looted and destroyed. This was over a sporting event.

After the 2006 Super Bowl, over 100 people were arrested for arson, theft, vandalism, looting and overturning cars.

The riot which broke out in Huntington Beach after the U.S. Open of Surfing was blamed on "unruly beachgoers." Eight people were arrested and several officers injured. Police in riot gear had to use tear gas to disperse the crowd of mostly white youth who were tipping over portable toilets and smashing storefront windows. Even though windows were smashed, looting occurred and were toilets tipped over, which sounds incredibly gross, they were called rowdy and mischievous. This is opposed to every riot involving blacks where they are called thugs who "destroy their own community."

Chapter 14

From the first, people were always interested in our children's origins. One preschooler demanded to know which baby came out of my stomach, "the brown boy or the yellow girl?" A young teenager shyly asked if I know my kids real parents, I wanted to ask if I looked like a holograph or what. Pinch me; see if I'm real. Believe me, if I wasn't real, I wouldn't have spent so much time potty-training a stubborn 3-year-old or stayed up all night waiting for a 17-year-old to come home. However, I'm not offended by the question. We know varying amounts about the birth families of our children. In reality, I want to know more. I want every one of my children to meet his or her birth family.

When they were younger our children had trouble with the question, "Do you know your "real" parents?" If someone asked about their biological parents or birth parents, my children understood the question and would respond, or, depending on their mood, pretend like no one had spoken. But when someone asked about "real," the children, for the most part, got confused. I'm the real one to them. I can be touched. I'm the one who yells. I'm the one they planned on running away from because they had to scrub the floor, and I'm the one who hides school backpacks in the closet where they belong. The opposite of real is pretend and if I were pretending to be a mom I'd certainly turn these sex talks over to the real parent.

When they were young, I tried to tell my children we are both real. I'm real and birth parents are real. These children may look more like their birth parents, but I read that animal noises book twenty-eight times in one day, so we both have a great stake in the child's development.

Actually adoption may be a better way to get children. When I look at the child I gave birth to, I often wonder if she is going to act like her aunt she resembles a little, or is that temper tantrum indicative of another relative, or will she. . . ? My other children were spared such speculation. From the start, I allowed them to just be who they are.

Chapter 15

As our children grew older, they understood better how people didn't see our family as we see it. At about age 6 and 7 each of them go through an awareness of his or her color and the color of all the siblings. After the initial exploration they have moved on to other interests and concerns. Not that the color isn't relevant, but like all things we live with daily, the color becomes familiar, common, ordinary, pointless and unoriginal as a topic. They just see each other as brothers and sisters.

While I was trying to get the house ready to sell so we could move to the Northwest, Garrett mentioned William and Keeley, both 5 years old at the time, had never played T-ball.

"You hated T-ball," I informed him. "You were horrible. You could throw the ball further than anyone on the team, but you kept forgetting where to throw the ball. You kept forgetting you were actually in a game."

"I know," he admitted. "But maybe you raised them to have a better attention span."

I doubted it, but I signed them up anyway.

I wasn't looking forward to the time commitment. And I was even less enthusiastic when I arrived at the first practice and saw their assigned coach.

"Seriously?" I thought. "This woman is not up to the task of managing a T-Ball team."

Five and 6-year-old kids are so inept at the game, fans on the sidelines have to voice-activate the players' every move.

"Swing!" the parents must yell after the pitcher has pitched a fake ball. Then the kid swings at the T where the real ball is precariously balanced. If by some stroke of luck the bat actually connects with the ball, then the player's parent must yell, "Run!"

A parent from the opposing team will then shout, "Catch!" to some kid who has removed her mitt and is contemplating her fingernail polish.

Some parents even jog ahead of the kid waving the clueless player on to the right base. I guess these parents figure if the child runs to third rather than first then the kid won't get a participation trophy at the end of the season. Parents should lighten up. Some of my older kids ran the wrong way on more than one occasion, and they still got a trophy.

My older children made mistakes and they had "real" coaches--coaches who had name-brand shoes and well-worn baseball gloves. What was going to happen to my younger kids? The coach assigned to their team was not a "real" coach. I was wondering if she had any clue how to voice-activate a team. She was too old and heavy to run. Between her polyester pants and white socks were two inches of even whiter skin. Her shoes were from an antiquated line of nursing orthotics. She didn't have a mitt, but she did have three coolers. THREE! Really? This is T-ball. Not a picnic.

She asked for help carrying her coolers. How had she gotten these things loaded into her van? They were incredibly heavy. None of the other T-ball parents had to verbalize their dismay. We only had to look at one another in disgust as we lugged our loads over to home plate where she told us to deposit them. Except for the little red cooler, it was placed at first base.

She lined the players up and opened a cooler. From it she lifted a water balloon and placed it on the T.

"Make it splash big," she told them. "And then run to first base by the cooler full of popsicles."

With an attention span unheard of in minor league T-ball, those kids spent two hours swinging and running the right way. When the larger coolers were empty, she gave them a Popsicle from the red cooler.

We played an entire season without a single kid running the wrong direction. And at the end of the season every kid got a trophy, but the biggest award should have gone to a woman who filled 400 balloons with water and improved the attention span of an entire team.

I tell our experience, because this woman was like so many individuals in our lives. She felt no different about William than she did about blonde Keeley or any of the other players. This woman loved children. In reality much of our life has been like this woman. Well, not exactly like this woman. Very few people tie that many water balloons. But there have been people who are totally nonplused by the color of my children and other humans.

This type of experience has happened over and over. Not with water balloons and orthotic nurses' shoes, but with coaches and teachers and friends who went way beyond what was expected.

A few years after my older three had graduated, I had reason to be in the high school. Jeanne, a secretary in the athletic office, stopped in midstride and twirled in the hall to come speak with me.

"How are the boys?" she asked. This woman had called our home more than once.

"Garrett has a fine for a lost book," Jeanne would say. "We can't clear him to play unless he pays it before tonight's game. If he'll stop in at the library and get a signed slip saying he's in the process of replacing the book, he can play."

"Colton has five tardies," Jeanne would call another day. "If he gets one more, he won't be cleared to play. I've told him. Maybe if we both warned him."

On this day, after all she had done for us, she was sincere when she requested they stop in and say "Hi" next time they were in town.

She treated them no different than any other. Lots of students got calls from her. The principal and the security officer, the track coach all genuinely wanting to know about the boys and their lives. Because these people cared.

William and Keeley's first athletic coach, their creative T-ball coach, wasn't there to be a hero or garner accolades. In reality, she didn't appear capable of producing quality ball players, but she gave a great start to anyone with potential, and gave a memorable experience to all the others. I didn't adopt children to be a hero or a savior. When I see pictures of us all together I examine the mother, who is me, and think how incapable I look to give them the start they need.

I suspect there were on occasion individuals (can you say "my children?") who looked at me and thought I brought just as much to the parenting field as the orthotic shod woman brought to the ball field. Certainly I'm no Sandra Bullock in the "Blind Side." I'm much more like our T-ball coach. Too old, too out of shape and too inexperienced to appear capable. But I've metaphorically filled all the water balloons I could find. Just as she did. I wasn't here to be a savior. I just showed up when everyone else was busy.

"Do you worry about your children bonding like siblings?" a woman asked me one day.

"Do bonded siblings fight?" I asked.

"Yes," she said.

"Then we're good," I assured her.

"But they also love and defend and support each other."

"Yeah, my kids do that, too," I said with a lot less conviction.

We had recently lined our kids up for a family photo. Two years earlier we had attempted the same thing, put them in matching shirts and insisted they smile for a photographer. The resulting photo hung on our wall as a reminder of the contention that results in trying to color coordinate five children.

Confidently we had thought the intervening 24 months would have matured us all to the point we could agree on a color scheme and sit close enough that a wide angle lens would not be necessary. We were overly optimistic.

"I think we should be allowed to show our individual and unique tastes," my oldest daughter suggested when I'd told the family about our group appointment. "We'll all wear what we want."

"I have a new shirt," 11-year-old Keeley chirped, excited about the prospect of wearing clothes I told her should be saved for school.

"It's ugly," Colton said with more conviction than you would expect from a brother who hadn't even seen the new addition to his sister's wardrobe.

"I'm good to go, Mom," Garrett said cheerfully when I asked if he'd like something new and unstained for this picture that would be a permanent record of our family unit. "It's all good."

He wore a white undershirt to the photo shoot.

At the time Colton was partial to black T-shirts with no collar, no buttons, and no pocket. Definitely no pockets.

"That's like just weird having a little pocket on your chest," Colton muttered. "Like what you going to stick in there, a little bottle of nose drops? Gross."

William wanted to go shopping for something new. Colton warned him not to get pockets.

Alexis decided to wait and see what "mood" struck her after she'd done her hair.

The photographer's smile looked more insincere than the ones the kids were displaying to the camera. They were standing in a rigid line with about six inches between each of them.

"Get closer together," he told them waving an arm. "You guys are a family." There appeared to be a question mark at the end of his statement.

"You on the end, in the white T-shirt," the photographer pointed. "Put your hand on your sister's shoulder."

"What for?" Garrett asked.

"Right there on her shoulder," the man behind his camera ignored my son's question.

The 15-year-old laid a stiff hand on his sister's shoulder.

"Don't pinch me," Colton yelled from the other side, jumping away from the group.

"I was putting my hand on your shoulder," Alexis said innocently. "Because we're a happy family that loves each other."

"Love me without touching me," the 13-year-old threatened.

The two youngest stood grinning stiffly at the camera. Their arms hung unbending on either sides of their bodies.

The camera man snapped a couple pictures recognizing how unappealing the arrangement was.

"Would you like something a bit more relaxed?" he finally suggested, looking around the park

"Let's do a pyramid," one of the kids said and within ten seconds they had agreed that the boys would be the base and the girls would climb on top. And that's the picture which hung on our wall for several years.

Chapter 16

"I just love black boys," the little high school junior giggled. She was pulling up on her prom dress, but then, not one to waste the effects of a good push-up bra, she pulled the material back down a couple inches. Examining herself in the reflection of the shining limousine, she seemed satisfied a sufficient expanse of cleavage was on display. Her shoes were platform heels that had a zipper to close three inches of lace covering her ankles. Nothing concealed the rest of her legs until the glittery, baby-blue satin appeared several inches above her knees. The short dress gave great exposure to a lot of bronzed skin. Apparently, she also wasn't a girl to waste the effects of several visits to a tanning bed.

"I love them, too," her friend agreed, carefully adjusting the bodice on her slightly less revealing gown. "They are sooooooo funny."

Prom traditions vary with area and schools, but where my teens attended high school "groups" went to prom together. If the planning had been done correctly, one member of the group had a large house with a circular driveway and some water feature which would be a picturesque background for the photos. And if they were really lucky, someone would fall in and the video would go viral. This never once happened when I showed up at numerous picture sessions. The best I ever got were the primping girls as they discussed my son and his friends.

I didn't know these two particular girls very well, but they did know I was mother to one of the "soooo funny" black boys.

"You're Colton's mom," one of them stated as I tried to slink away, pretending I hadn't heard their comments.

"Yes," I said pleasantly. I didn't know what to do with my face when the other girl giggled again and said, "So you really do love black boys."

Should I look amused? Confused? Should I nod in agreement? I couldn't look down, I'd be staring directly into her cleavage.

Her statement came across as a little creepy and I wasn't sure exactly what to say.

I personally don't love all black boys in about the same proportion as I don't love all white boys.

Are they all funny? No, there was nothing funny about them doing doughnuts in the parking lot which resulted in bending the frame of Colton's little Honda Civic. There was nothing funny about the sweaty smell which followed them after a football game. But those statements could be made for any color of kid.

Can't you just love Colton or Garrett or William or does he have to be black?

I looked around the prom group gathering on the newly cut grass. Most of the girls were tugging on something. Even transformed as they were in their tuxes, the boys were more familiar to me than the girls, simply because boys were the ones in my living room screaming at the TV, or falling asleep on one of the couches.

Not too long before this prom, I'd threatened a couple of them. If I smelt marijuana in Colton's car one more time, I'd sell the little blue vehicle. They could use another means of transportation for their illegal substance.

"It's not our weed," Colton assured me. "We're just keeping it for a couple of our friends."

"And no kid has ever said that before," I said scornfully. "You can pee in a cup to prove it's not yours."

"Sure," he said confidently and then discussed whether second-hand smoke would give a positive reading.

"It's going to be legal soon," one friend promised me. "Then no one will care who smokes it."

"You're not 21," I told him. "And it's my car."

"It's Colton's."

"Like he made payments on it," I said.

"You won't sell it," another kid sounded confident as he got a can of juice out of my freezer.

"I will," I promised him.

"Where's a pitcher?" he asked.

"In the dishwasher."

"Thanks," he said and proceeded to mix a drink from frozen concentrate.

"You want a sandwich?" I asked. "There's meat in the fridge."

"You got any of that potato soup?" he asked.

"It's gone. I'll make some this weekend," I promised. "I'm serious about the car."

"I like that pasta salad, too?" he hinted.

Within a month I had to follow through on selling Colton's car.

"It reeks," I told him one night.

"No one smoked in there," my son assured me.

"But I can smell weed," I accused him.

"You won't be able to find it," he grinned.

Why was this kid joking about hiding an illegal substance in his car? We weren't having an Easter egg hunt.

"So you admit it's in there?"

"Find it," he challenged me.

I took that challenge. Starting with under the seats, glove compartment, then under the spare tire. I pulled interior walls out and sniffed a lot trying to isolate the smell.

Colton laughed.

He was right. I personally never located this stash of marijuana. A friend of ours who is a "car guy" knew exactly where to look—the tail lights.

To our chagrin, our son never seemed particularly upset about sharing the family van as a means of transportation. He handled the situation with typical cheerfulness. Now he could haul even more friends.

"Be mad, I sold your car," I wanted to say. "Don't turn every disciplinarian situation into something good." I understood how frustrated his fifth-grade teacher was when he enjoyed picking up garbage.

Another thing which was frustrating about the illegal substance is the boys' supplier was often a father.

For you parents who have never had occasion to have your child drug tested, I'm sorry you missed this particular bonding experience. There's something unique about labs and results. During our wait for Colton's, we read a poster about DNA testing. We requested a pamphlet and decided this was something he wanted. Eventually, a kit was ordered. Marijuana led us to find out more about his biological heritage.

Chapter 17

As a first grader, I carefully monitored a bag of miniature marshmallows my mom left on a storage room shelf. I didn't have the courage to tear the plastic wrapping, but was prepared to taste a few if she was foolish enough to leave an open bag sitting around.

One day a corner of the bag had been torn, and several of the little round puffy sweets were scattered on the shelf. Immediately, I knew my younger sister had done this deed. And like the idiot I believed her to be, she had only eaten about half of each small marshmallow. Dim-witted though my sibling was, I didn't want her disciplined. So I ate all the left-over halves.

The amygdalae in my brain are responsible for my ability to so clearly remember this long-ago event. These almond-shaped groups of neurons perform a primary role in the memory of emotional events. Our most vivid autobiographical memories tend to be of emotional incidents.

So what emotion is attached to this event in the storage room?

My sister hadn't opened that bag and eaten those marshmallows. Mice had. What an emotional shock to find out I was the dimwitted one. Emotionally charged memories are preserved in greater detail than more neutral memories, but they may also be subject to distortion.

When my children get together, they revive events from their childhood. Sometimes I wonder what emotional component is causing them to remember. At the same time I recognize their memory of the event and my memory of the same incident isn't always consistent.

All the kids were still in elementary school, when I strung a 100-foot extension cord under the garage door and out to my children's fort. They were playing in a dry gully just beyond the lush green grass of our front yard. The fort was furnished with a couple logs for chairs and a level spot for my old electric frying pan. Huddled together, the siblings were using unwashed sticks to spear sausages off of the electric skillet which would barely heat to warm.

To hear my kids reminisce about this early morning breakfast in the dirt, you'd think we'd spent every Saturday morning impersonating hobos who had discovered extension cords and electrical outlets. The recollections sounded like they had been treated to a tantalizing variety of foods rather than a package of pre-cooked sausage and a gallon of milk that was due to expire at noon.

"Remember when we used to cook breakfast in our fort?" one of my children will say.

"Yeah, that was always so much fun," another will reply.

"We always had the best sausages," another memory-impaired child will add.

We did it once. Once. That's all. I rolled the cord up and never plugged it into a frying pan again. However, I don't tell them that. What kind of idiot parent would inform their children that those happy times were so rare?

Even more vivid than purely emotional events is our recall of negative events. Fear and sadness are negative emotions which increase activity in a part of the brain linked to memories. Which is a good thing if you are a caveman. Forgetting the difference between a saber tooth and a jack rabbit may have serious consequences.

One event which combines both emotion and fear is teaching a teenager to drive.

"Where did my little boy go?" we sentimentally reminisce as he slides confidently into the driver's seat and begins the pre-driving check of complaining about why the seat is so close to the steering wheel and finding music designed to maximize my discomfort.

There is diversity of opinion about Colton's ability to drive. I think he needs to slow down, pay attention and stop texting or eating a Carl's Junior Hamburger. He, on the other hand, thinks he can avoid any accident just because he has such fast reflexes and a full-time guardian angel.

In all the times he and I rode together, I was only in one "driving incident" with him. This incident was insignificant enough not to be considered an "accident." He was pulling into a driveway and hit the mail box.

"Why'd they hide the mailbox?" Colton asked in disgust.

"I don't think they exactly were trying to hide it," I suggested looking at the scratches on the front of our white F150 pickup. "I think the tree grew up around the mailbox because no one lives here."

"That's messed up. Don't be hiding stuff," he grumbled as I checked to see what type of damage had been done to the mail box.

"I don't think there's any major repairs needed," I mused.

"I'm not paying to fix a mailbox that was hidden," Colton argued. "I couldn't even see it."

"But, you shouldn't have hit the tree," I submitted.

"I didn't hit the tree," he countered. "Just the branches. Hitting branches isn't a problem."

"It is if there's a mailbox hidden behind it." I answered.

"So you admit they hid it?" he said effortlessly, lowering a lawn mower from the truck bed.

A couple years earlier, Garrett had applied for a business license and the State of Washington took his money and said he was now the proud owner of a company called "Mighty Men Mowing." The 17-year-old hired a few football friends and they were mighty men mowing private yards as well as an increasing number of bank-owned properties, homes which had been repossessed.

Garrett moved on in life. Colton took over the business license and a route of nearly 100 houses. However, with only a learner's permit, the younger brother needed an adult sitting beside him while he drove. If I didn't win mother-of-the-year for that I never will—teaching him to drive, as well as mowing lawns in rain and heat, should have qualified me for at least an honorable mention.

I just looked up a spreadsheet we kept for tax purposes. Every lawn we mowed or repossessed house we cleaned is recorded. We went to 1,158 properties that season. Colton didn't drive to all of them, but probably at least 80 percent. This means he mowed approximately 80 lawns every week during the summer, sometimes 30 in a day. Sometimes only 20 because he had to be back for football practice. One time he hit a mail box and I wrote about this particular yard. Not the other 700 times he pulled into a driveway without producing new scratches.

This is just one example of our human tendency to remember the negative. Logically we must pay particular attention to potentially threatening information. Preserving bad memories is undoubtedly an evolutionary tactic to protect against future life-threatening or negative events.

There's another property Colton and I mowed together which he remembers and I remind him of periodically, especially if there are people around. The house had a large back yard which reached down to the edge of a wetland. Apparently this particular wetland was a very popular resort location for snakes of all sizes and temperament. I'd see dozens of the reptiles slither ahead of me as I pushed one mower. In horror, Colton watched them wiggle toward him and his mower which was also stirring up occupants of the grass he was attempting to trim. For a while he felt somewhat inoculated from these frightening creepy crawlers by tiptoeing through the grass. Eventually, he gave up all pretense of bravery and ran to the driveway. From his safe spot on the cement he promised he'd personally mow every lawn for the rest of the day, if I would just finish this one.

While traveling around together, especially as we pulled into driveways, I remembered Colton's previous miscalculation with where he put the bumper of our truck. Consequently, I persistently worried about him hitting another tree or crashing into something. He, on the other hand, wasn't as emotionally involved in the mailbox, therefore he spent his travel time finding the right song.

Even though I continually focused on the potentially lethal results his driving might have produced, he was never in an accident which produced "bodily injury." There was the time he was drifting right after a snow storm and we had to straighten the frame of his 20-year old Honda.

"It's not my fault this car can't take bumping up against the curb," he said. "You should get me a bigger car."

"With more power?" his dad asked. "I don't think so."

No law enforcement officer ticketed him for the "drifting" incident. In fact, he wasn't ever ticketed during high school. Oh, he was stopped nearly two dozen times for speeding/reckless driving/other stupid stuff. This does not surprise anyone. What does surprise us all is how he was never fined. His ticket avoidance was not a result of him driving slowly. He doesn't ease away from a stop light and settle into the flow of traffic. He would gun the ancient Honda from the light and quickly shifted through its five gears, racing ahead of traffic while weaving through slower vehicles.

"I know how to talk to cops," Colton bragged when we wondered why he never had to appear in traffic court. "I'm just good that way."

"Yeah, you're good," we agreed, our tone just this side of sarcastic.

Although I asked for details about these encounters with the law, he wasn't particularly enthusiastic about providing specifics. "You know it was on that road going to Pleasant Valley, going over the hills. The po-po stopped me, I kept my hands on the wheel, gave him my license, called him sir. He gave me a warning. Said to drive safe. I was going to go out and drive dangerously, but then he said to 'drive safe' so I felt inspired to maneuver carefully. Like when you tell me to study hard, I never go study soft."

In college Colton finally received a ticket.

He enthusiastically told us every detail. We heard a lengthy discussion (can you say tirade) about how cops should be doing something better than picking up people going 10 miles over the speed limit. Okay, maybe 20, but there was nothing erratic about the driving and there are so many problems in the world.

"Why waste time on a careful driver trying to be a responsible citizen by getting to work on time so he can pay taxes?" Colton warmed to his topic. "The taxes needed to pay salaries to, uh, let me think, salaries to the policemen. They make bank all because I have to get to work on time."

Certainly, this bad experience (and the subsequent loss of a day's wages) had more of an impression on him than those multiple good experiences he had with police officers. Just like the one time he hit a mailbox had a more lasting impression on me than the 800 driveways he successfully navigated past mailboxes and tree branches.

For the speeding ticket, Colton never suggested racial profiling. He knew he was, in fact, speeding. Later, however, he was on a motorcycle and a campus police officer followed him. The two of them formed a short parade creeping 25 miles per hour over much of the campus. Finally, Colton gunned the bike, flipped a U-turn, went down an alley and lost the officer. The incident does sound eerily like an episode which could have ended badly. Fortunately, Colton remembered what could happen. He didn't let his guard down because of the many good experiences.

For Colton's survival he must remember there are those who would shoot more quickly because he is black. For our sanity, we also need to remember the many officers who are honestly there to make society safer and don't want to randomly give tickets to young boys who don't yet have a sense of their own mortality.

The U.S. Youth Soccer Regional Championship was being held in Boise, Idaho, one summer, a huge event which attracted players, parents and coaches from all over the United States. Colton was in the community with no place to stay. We'd had a family reunion in the mountains above Idaho's capital city. A popular impromptu activity at the reunion was to stand around Colton's motorcycle and marvel. How had this threadbare tire carried him up the gravel road without blowing out? He now had an appointment to have the tires replaced. Luckily his mom had paid for the new tires, and, because she likes the way his face looks, threatened him. "Don't ride home without new tires."

We went home, unaware his friend couldn't accommodate him for an overnight stay, or, because of the soccer tournament, there would be no hotels, cheap or otherwise.

"I'll just sleep in the park," he told me on the phone. "There are other people doing it. Which is probably why there are so many cops around," he considered. "But that's the good thing about being black--they won't see me. I'll try not to smile."

"Don't sleep in the park, Colton."

He didn't; he tried to ride home. The tire blew just before the Bliss, Idaho, exit. He survived (his bike not so unscathed) and hopefully he would have survived a night in the park unscathed. However, the thought of him curled up next to his bike frightened me. Probably no more than this would have frightened any mother regardless of her kid's color. Yet, because of so many vivid negative images, I felt he would be seen as less friendly than a different color of kid.

Even though our brains are more adept at storing the negative events, we must hold on to the good memories.

Definitely as a group, we must be concerned about prejudice, but as an individual I must tell my sons that there is hatred for a lot of groups, so don't get yourself up every morning looking for the hatred. Don't get up and think, "Oh, someone is going to hate me today so I have to be on the defense."

Chapter 18

Regardless of their color, there is a relationship which develops between parents, especially parents of high schoolers, when they spend every weekend cheering their children on to sports victory and complaining about the coaching when their children's team doesn't win. Marsha and I had spent football, basketball and track seasons together, cheering and complaining. We ate together and shivered through day-long track meets. We hugged one another when the boys hugged one another after a win. We watched our boys fight back tears when a false start out of the blocks disqualified the relay team from going on to the finals. We fought back our own tears.

One year we spent three days together at a state track meet. We shared a hotel room, shared meals and endured long hours on cold bleachers. After one particular event I went down to get a picture.

There was no room on the cement steps for me to squeeze my backside, but I forced my body down right next to a woman with a smaller backside. And lots better hair. And her nails were also very professionally done. But my camera was better. She had a cell phone she was aiming at the podium. I had a zoom lens.

Great nails, better fitting jeans, stylish hair, tiny waist vs zoom lens. I win.

Colton was on the podium for taking first place. (Actually he took second, but, hey, it could easily have been first--milliseconds, you know.) Her son was standing in the fourth-place spot. So I win again.

They were placing medals around the boys' necks when a man approached and told us we couldn't sit on the steps and take pictures.

"Gotta move," he insisted like a guy who is in the habit of giving orders and having those orders obeyed. Maybe ex-military.

"Now!" he commanded.

This 6'4" guy looked exactly like a male who had probably won a lot of athletic competitions before he gained an extra 15 pounds. He had a staff hat and an official jacket which suggested he had been commissioned by some track and field organizing committee to actually keep people off those cold cement steps situated right in front of where the winners were going to stand.

I would have gotten up and moved, but I was somewhat hampered by my zoom lens and the other mothers with whom we were sharing a cozy position.

"You have to move!" he was irritated and arrogant. We all shifted to allow one another enough space to stand. Except, the smallest, best dressed, amongst us didn't move. Keeping her eyes on the podium and without lowering her cell phone, she spoke.

"You," she said her voice firm. "You will have to bodily remove me. I drove four hours to get here. I slept in a hotel with a million and a half kids who never went to bed. I spent all my cash to get into this meet. And your concession stand doesn't take debit cards. I WILL NOT move until I get a picture of my son on that podium."

Like a practiced protestor, I looped my arm through the arm of this perfect stranger and said, "I'm with her."

The man tucked his proverbial tail between his proverbial legs and edged away.

Authority and power versus moms. We win.

I may have sat there with the other women in solidarity, but I didn't scream or yell my son's name. I've always been very careful about not drawing attention to the fact he is my son. In our region, everyone knows him and who his mother is, but when we travel to Seattle and Tacoma for state meets or games, he is known because his times are competitive. He is not known as the black kid from the white family. I always assumed he wanted to keep that anonymity.

When Marsha and I travel together, her daughters often come. They scream and cheer for their brother, Jamariay, as well as Colton. Colton especially acknowledges them. Waving to them in the bleachers as he stretches on the track. I am quiet. He actually acknowledges me more than I do him, because he gets hungry, and I have money.

One night I called Marsha and her husband wanting to know if I could visit. We were friends. I assumed she would honestly tell me how she felt about black children going to white families.

I love Marsha. Her husband is the kindest, mildest man. I know Colton respects him. They were gracious as I sat in their living room most of one afternoon. We talked about sports and our boys and black culture verses white culture. We talked about how they would sooner black children go to black homes. Yet, a child should have loving parents rather than not have a home.

We talked about the things black men should teach their sons. Some of those things can't be taught by a white man.

We talked about the different discipline styles she saw in our home versus her home. The couple felt I allowed Colton to say disrespectful things to me they would never allow from their own son. They then explained how respectful my son was while in their home.

Not at any point did I feel defensive. These are the kindest most wonderful people. There was never a point where I wanted to stop them and protest until the end when someone mentioned whites trying to be saviors to the blacks. Going on volunteer missions and draping themselves in little black kids.

My boys are my sons. I was never on a mission to be anyone's Savior. We took three little guys who needed a home. I wasn't here to be part of the solution or part of the problem or part of any movement. There was never a conscious moment when I said, "Oh, the black community can't deal with these children. I will rise up and save them." Didn't say it. Didn't think it. If anything, they have taught me more than I'll ever teach them.

I just tried to metaphorically load four coolers with water balloons to start them off on a journey. To improve their attention span and get them going in the right direction.

Chapter 19

Typical days for us were the same as typical days for others. We dug fries out of the back seat. We were in a rut as to what to fix for supper. The bills are too high. No one wants to eat stew. The healthy cereal grows stale in the cabinet and during those high school and middle school days someone always had a couch cushion over his or her head when we were trying to have a family scheduling meeting.

Some people might have stared at our family, but most of the world is too busy to care about us or our life. Others were our good friends. Yes, there are those who would burn crosses and paint swastikas on their forearms. When they do the newspapers will report it and most of the population will shake their collective head and murmur about the rise in prejudice.

Skinhead groups will shoot blacks at bus stops and I will fear again. Black youth will be killed by cops and protestors will march. Some idiot will hang a noose from a tree of a prestigious university. These incidents happen. They are reality. But in that reality is also another less reported more subtle reality. The little girl next door who played with my youngest son, insisted on including a black doll in her expensive collection of dolls. Hate is projected loudly and violently. However, there appears to be a quieter group that seems to be learning to accept more. Or at least to care less one way or another. So if the violence is more apparent, the acceptance is quieter.

Acceptance comes from people like the woman who tied 400 water balloons. If she has a bias, her kindness overrode the default belief she might have had.

Probably the overall most damaging prejudice is the subtle feeling so many of us have about races and people we don't know. This is generally a quiet, almost unconscious belief another group isn't as good as my group. That narrow-mindedness is alive and well.

As I write things people have said, I fear in some way this adds to division. Let me explain. At a recent conference, I heard an older, intelligent, beautiful black woman mention how offended she was because someone had watched some horrible news footage from Africa and then asked her if she wasn't grateful her ancestors had been brought to the United States.

"How can I be grateful?" she asked indignantly.

The question was not asked out of prejudice. Hearing her indignation made me scared to have a conversation with her. What questions might I ask which I don't recognize are insulting to her? I was going to go speak with this woman, but now I am nervous about doing so. What if I say something that she finds offensive?

Several others speakers gave examples of "insensitive" comments.

Colton was pragmatic about the effect these types of comments would have on him personally.

"She's really cute," Colton said once of a girl he had met right before he participated in a panel on adoption. "But now she won't speak to me."

"You were talking before," I reminded him.

"But now she'll be scared to talk to me, because she'll be scared to 'offend' me," he explained. "People always avoid you if they think they might not say the right thing."

I have a brother who lives in a supported facility for the mentally ill. People ask questions which could be considered insensitive about his situation. But they are not asking these questions out of rudeness or with a lack of compassion. Instead they have not dealt with mental illness.

When I had miscarriages, comments were not always sensitive. My friend has an autistic son. There are hurtful comments.

How many things do I say to people because I don't understand the situation? I've said things to my children and they have responded angrily, "You don't understand."

They are right. Understanding is hard. I don't want to be angry because someone doesn't understand me. If comments are only motivated by a lack of understanding and not by prejudice, let us move on. And if they are motivated by prejudice, I can't do anything. I can only change myself.

The Tacoma Mall has a barber shop which is pretty much dedicated to ethnic haircuts. We travel to Tacoma regularly for state sporting events and the boys plan their haircuts around being there.

"Oh, no," I said when a game got cancelled. "William will have to get his haircut in Portland."

Our good friend who loves our boys and would never ever consider herself prejudiced asked what I meant. I explained.

"Oh, yeah," she said. "They do have problems up there."

Her brain jumped immediately from black barber shop to "problems."

This is one good woman's default.

Chapter 20

I don't know what this book is about. Is it about adoption or about racial adoption? I started writing this commentary when the kids were in grade school. I have trashed significant portions of my cute little stories. At the time, I thought black and adoption didn't matter. People would say, wait until they are older. And I thought these naysayers were crazy because I loved my kids and they loved me.

It turns out these naysayers were, in fact, right about some things. These people weren't so crazy after all. This thing called race does matter, but in other ways, it has ceased to matter as much. You may notice this narrative is kind of heavy on kid experiences and not so much on their experiences when they grow older. There's a reason for this few years of silence about their lives. Simply put, they don't want you to know about those teen years.

Things change. Your relationship with your children change. When my little group of five were young I was the funniest woman on the planet.

I would ask my children if they knew what color a burp was. When I told them it was "Burple" they laughed uproariously.

"Tell us more jokes?" they begged eagerly.

"What do you get when you mix a rabbit with a snake?" I asked.

The answer is a "jump rope," and I'll have you know my children were very amused by that little riddle.

They also thought I was the most generous person in the world when I would drag a garden hose into the laundry room and run hot water out into their blue wading pool. This was a luxurious addition to the cold, outside tap water that they typically swam in.

"This is the life," my 5-year-old daughter sighed contentedly as she leaned back into the 12 inches of tepid water. Her two younger brothers readily agreed, and I was the best mom in the land.

During this same period of time was when they would stand mesmerized as I typed without looking at my fingers.

"How do you do that?" they would say in reverent admiration.

"Ah," I speak modestly. "A lot of people can type without looking."

"Do my name," one would politely request, and without hesitation, I would hit all seven letters of the child's name without looking at the keyboard even once.

Things have changed in the last few years. For example, the reviews on my standup comedy routine turned really sour.

"You're not even funny," they'd tell me regularly.

But then I didn't think they were so hilarious either when they insisted that being asked if there were dishes under their beds constituted an invasion of privacy.

Now as they move out and actually become successful without me washing their dishes, they also want to work their way through the world.

When he was 16-years-old, Colton and I took a road trip to see his sister in college. When I suggested this trip, he had asked, "Can I drive the whole way?"

"Well, part of the way," I thought about my nerves for eight hours at freeway speeds.

"Okay, I'll go."

We had been driving less than an hour when I told him to stop texting.

"I'm not texting," he had insisted. "I'm reading a text."

"Stop reading," I said.

"Your turn," he said.

"You've only driven 40 miles."

"It's boring," he said looking up at the long stretch of freeway. "And I hear Angry Birds calling."

When a teenager is responding to the call of mad fowl, some parents would deem this evidence enough that said 16-year-old should be relieved from driving duty.

"The mad chickens will have to wait," I responded calmly.

"Angry Birds," he corrected disgustedly. "You know that. Don't try to be funny."

He was right. I did know this new game was called "Angry Birds."

"Check your blind spot," I said as he changed lanes to pass a semi.

"This is the only fun part about driving," he said as the speedometer rose to 85 mph, and I held tightly to the handle over my head.

"Slow down," I said.

"You have to get around semis fast," he explained casually.

"Why?"

"You can't just be chilling by semis or you'll run into them," he continued. "I learned that playing 'Need for Speed."

"This isn't a game."

"I know," he said and muttered something about how no one ever complained about blind spots during the racing game. Then he started hearing the Angry Birds again.

"The pigs have all the eggs locked up in the beach house," he complained. "You have to have the right angle to get the bird past the pig fishing for sharks."

"I'll drive."

Without signaling, he pulled over.

We switched places. He strapped on his seatbelt, made some remark about my erratic driving, then pulled out his iPod and clicked to the new app he'd downloaded before we'd left home. I could hear the squawk of Angry Birds. Carefully the boy calculated the right angle needed to sling a bird toward egg-stealing pigs.

The semi we'd just passed raced ahead of us.

Colton glanced up, "Now you can have fun passing him."

Five years later we were on another road trip together. Some things had changed. He no longer played Angry Birds. He had decided not to play football in college since none of the schools he was interested in had offered him a scholarship. He had been through military training and claimed he had now cleaned more bathrooms than I had.

He may have matured, but he was just as distractible as he'd been since birth, so when he started talking about how race had affected him in high school I asked if I could write down what he said. I knew if he spoke, he would be honest. I also knew he would only be in a reflective mood for a very short period of time.

We'd been traveling over slushy cold roads since early morning. My laptop was in the trunk, but I knew this kid. If we stopped and got the computer his attention would be directed elsewhere.

"Four star reporter there," Colton said, taking his eyes off the road just long enough to nod at my cardboard.

My makeshift writing tablet was a brown piece of cardboard which I'd ripped from a box in the back seat. The rough texture reduced my poor penmanship to barely legible. However Colton didn't appreciate being quoted incorrectly, and he was willing to talk, so I needed to write precisely what he said.

I'd told him I was writing a commentary on our family called Motherhood in Black and White.

"Oh that's about adoption. Wow. I just figured that out," Colton said staring through the windshield as semis splattered cold snow up on us. "Wow. I thought at first it was like black and white like on the page."

"Yes, I've been asked to be involved in a conference about adoption. Would you like to go with me, you know, if it fits your schedule?"

"Heck no. Well maybe. Heck no. What would I say? Oh, man, I'd freak them out. 'Hey, guys, don't adopt it's horrible. They'd all just get up and leave. No, maybe I'd come. If I have time. If it fits my schedule. Do they feed you at something like that? Is it real food or just like cookies?

See how he gets distracted.

"So is being adopted horrible?" I asked, knowing whatever answer he gave would come from the mood he was in at the present.

"No," he said, preoccupied with reaching outside and flipping the windshield wipers to remove accumulated ice.

"We need wiper fluid," he muttered.

"We're out?"

"Yea, this morning I thought maybe it was frozen and so it wouldn't work. But we've been driving for hours. It's not frozen. Let's stop and get more."

I agreed. "The semis splash so much we can hardly see."

He pushed on the gas and the car surged forward on the three inches of slush. "Then I won't let them pass," he said.

"Slow down," I said.

"We're okay," he ignored my advice.

"Slow down," I said again.

He didn't. He was young and invincible. That's why military recruiters target 18- and 19-year-olds. Boys this age think they will beat the odds and come home whole, sane and saying "oorah" with authority.

We drove a few miles in silence except for the tires spinning too quickly over icy roads.

"So you would tell people not to adopt?" I asked. I still had my cardboard. I was determined to fill the rough surface with insightful insights.

"Yea," he said. "I mean it hasn't been so great for you."

"Yes, it has."

"I don't think I would have wanted to raise me," he said. "You're getting wrinkles and gray hair. You'd be rich without us. I mean just think of it."

"So you're not talking about how you feel being adopted, but how I feel."

I think he nodded.

"But people coming want to know how you feel about being adopted not how you think I feel about you being adopted.

"This is too complicated," he said and then jerked the wheel scaring me as he exited. "We've got to get some windshield washing fluid."

Surprisingly, he continued the conversation once we were back on the freeway.

"I didn't know I was black for a while," he said. "I mean I knew my colors and all, but I didn't know it meant something."

"When did you know?" I asked.

"I don't know," he said thoughtfully. "Sometime before we moved to Portland, but more after that. Rylie in my third-grade class. Everyone got us mixed up and he wasn't exactly the brightest kid on the planet. People expected us to be just alike."

For a minute I didn't have anything to write on my cardboard and then Colton spoke again.

"But people expect you to be certain things when you're black. And you can go weeks without doing the thing they expect and then you do something and they are all, 'Wow. That's just like the black guy on TV.' It's like stereotype. You're supposed to listen to certain music. I didn't even like that kind of music. But I started listening because it was expected. People see your color first. They expect you to act like what they think your color acts."

"And how is that?" I asked hoping to get more examples than music.

"I don't know," he said irritably. Which doesn't mean he doesn't know.

"I don't know" means he doesn't want to vocalize what he does know. Or he's just tired of talking.

Colton always knows. He always has an opinion. So "I don't know" means we're not having this discussion. Instead we talked about blind spots, the muddy windshield and why he should slow down. Kind of the same conversation we'd had five years before.

Chapter 21

"When I meet people, I don't see nationality. I always reserve judgment until I know how they act and what they do," one man told me just before he went out and walked on water.

Okay, I didn't actually see him walking on water any more than I actually believe he "always reserves judgment."

Verna Myers, a diversity advocate, spoke of her own unconscious bias. In a TEDxBeaconStreet presentation, she describes traveling on a plane when the voice of a woman pilot comes over the PA. Myers admits to being so excited.

"Yes, women, we are rocking it. We are now in the stratosphere," Myers cheered inwardly.

However, when the flight experienced turbulence the woman's first thought was, "I hope she can drive . . . Female pilot: awesome. But it appears that when things get funky and a little troublesome, a little risky, I lean on a bias that I didn't even know that I had. You know, fast-moving planes in the sky, I want a guy. That's my default. Men are my default. Who is your default? Who do you trust? Who are you afraid of? Who do you implicitly feel connected to? Who do you run away from?"

Watch the full presentation at Ted Talks in which Myers suggests violence and black men are so much a part of our national psyche, that even young black men are scared of young black men.

Of course, people say they don't judge. We don't want to admit we have a default for who we want flying the plane, running the country or playing on our basketball team. When you first meet Colton, aren't you more likely to want him on your basketball team than on your debate team? Until you know him, you have to make up stories about him and these stories come from preconditioned responses.

Myers, who is black, suggests we stop pretending not to see color, religion, nationality and all the other things which divide us. Instead we should move toward these differences and have authentic relationships with those who are substantially different from us. "Build the type of relationship which actually causes you to see the whole person." This invitation is extended to everyone--the individuals in the majority and those individuals in the minorities.

So let's suppose my friend, in fact, was so perfect, he could walk on water as well as never judge. For him, his perfection meant writing or discussing prejudice was not worth his time, effort or energy. But for those of us who will admit to an unconscious bias, we recognize none of us walk on water. We are programmed by our media and past experience to judge others. We have a default of who we feel connected to and who we want to run away from.

As human beings we are neurologically hardwired to seek people resembling ourselves. We start creating cliques as soon as we appreciate what approval feels like. We connect on any level we can—music, religion, race, gender, sexual preference, the town we grew up in, our hobbies. We love to be in an environment which reinforces our personal choices.

My father used to tell stories. Absolute lies with no basis in reality. The only time he articulated these tall tales was when we were traveling. Excluding drive time, he was a pretty honest guy.

For a while, I believed his lies. His narratives were impressively detailed and told with confident authority.

"He's hurrying to get home," Dad would say when the red sedan darted in front of us forcing my father to brake. "His wife just called him at work. He puts sprinkler pipes together for a living. Last week they were putting up a pivot and he fell. He got hurt, but he's tough and hasn't complained. Now he has to hurry home because his wife is crying. Their dog ran away. It's a good dog, too except that part about drooling. I wouldn't have a dog which drools and there he is hurrying home to find his. Can't understand some people."

If a van pulled into the lane without signaling, dad knew this woman was normally a considerate individual, but a bit distracted. It's her son's birthday and she's baking him his favorite cake and she's burnt stuff before. Hopefully she'll get home before that cake in the oven burns.

There were lots of guys on the freeway who were hurrying home to do chores. Some of them had hungry milk cows waiting, mooing so loudly the neighbors had started complaining. Other drivers were concerned about the water freezing up on their horse trough.

"Can't blame a man for worrying about his riding horse," my dad might say.

A child can't help but be impressed when one man knows every driver and where they are headed. When I discovered all these scenarios were totally fabricated, the feeling was similar to discovering

I was sharing marshmallows with a mouse. He was just making up stories to humanize these drivers. They weren't jerks who should be flipped off, but individuals with stories.

Even though I now know many of the inconsiderate drivers on the road are just that, inconsiderate drivers, I still wonder who is hurrying home to bake a cake or feed a hungry horse. When we don't know people, we have to make up stories about them. Often these stories we make up are less than accurate and based on scenarios handed us by media. And like dad, intentions might be good, but outcomes less predictable.

Chapter 22

A social worker called us during the middle of November 1994 and asked if we would take Colton. There were legal complications and as those issues were sorted out, I had a few weeks to consider this step. I amassed as much research as I could find about biracial families and adoptions. At the time, I read a study which suggested the only truly non-prejudiced people are individuals who were raised in a biracial home or with siblings of another color. But, of course, I was the exception. I had no preconceived racial biases.

We moved on purpose, from the rural setting to an urban area with much more diversity. With diversity comes one-way streets and greyhound bus stops that are hidden away where I can't find them. Which was the reason I was in downtown Portland past midnight, in full panic mode.

I had printed directions for finding the bus stop, because this was before cheap GPS units or smart phones. I was completely confused by the bus lanes and one-way streets. Aborting my trip was not an option. My brother, who has severe challenges, was visiting us. He'd gotten on a Greyhound bus several hours earlier and he would be arriving within a few minutes. What he would do once he disembarked from his 18-hour trip without finding a familiar face is anyone's guess.

There was a surprising amount of pedestrian activity on the streets in these hours before twilight. A cop car totally ignored the middle-aged woman in a minivan timidly rolling along, going the wrong way on a one-way street. Instead the officer was watching one particular group. Silently, I begged the policeman to ticket me if he wanted, just, please, stop and give me instructions to the bus station.

At home my family was sleeping. Unaware, I was scared about not knowing where to go just as I was making a shocking discovery about how prejudiced I really was. Frantically, looking around for someone who could give me instructions, I didn't hail two black men crossing the street directly in front of me. Instead I checked to make sure the doors on my minivan were still locked.

"They probably don't know where the bus stop is," I mollified myself. Nonetheless, I recognized in myself the knee-jerk reaction of fearing young black men.

Within a few minutes, I did roll down my window and ask for directions. In defense of myself, a six-foot man stepping off the curb in stilettos while fixing his bra strap simply doesn't feel threatening. Especially if this crossdressing man has a purple feather boa.

Ten years later I was in the same area, only this time, I'd parked the car and was walking. Granted, the hour was a little more conventional, about midnight. I was now much more familiar with the streets, except I was still lost. The GPS on my phone indicated I was at the right building to meet my friends, but the name on the building was wrong. Three black teenagers were standing at the corner and without concern or hesitation I moved toward them, uttered a swift "Excuse me" and then asked the little group why I was not finding my location.

Like you, my life is on the phone. I can't remember my kids' phone numbers because I just punch favorites. All the best pictures are stored in this electronic device as well as my schedule and, of course, the GPS. Yet, I felt no qualms handing the valuable device to a young man and saying, "See, it says I'm right here. Do you know where I should be?"

Prejudices fade with familiarity. It's hard to be frightened of a kid who looks similar to Colton's friend, AJ. Under the right circumstances, AJ could be dangerous, I suppose. He was hazardous to the transmission of our Nissan truck. When I tried to teach him to drive a stick, he killed the little pickup a dozen times just getting out of the driveway. Kids who show such humility trying to master a clutch don't feel threatening. How can I be frightened when these boys in Portland look so much like Jamariay who sends me his English papers to proof, drools when he falls asleep on our living room couch and is a fan of my potato soup?

There is no greater potential for violence in Colton's black friends than there is in his white friends. Certainly, I'm not advising driving to downtown Portland and engaging with the gangs who roam the streets at three in the morning. Instead, my astonished awareness comes from realizing how a decade had changed me. I now know their stories. How fortunate I am to have known, not only my sons, but their friends. And appreciated them—except the marijuana in the taillights and a couple other habits age has remedied.

Chapter 23

I actually started recording stories about my children back when they were in grade school. I wrote less as they got older and my parenting ineptness became more evident. There are myriad examples of my incompetency. When I was trying to be the best mom in the land and put warm water in their pool from the laundry room, I ran the hot water in and got sidetracked. The pool was half full of scalding water before I got the cold hose. Nobody got scalded, but there was a perfect round ring in the grass burnt from the water.

There have been other times I'm not proud of what I did. But in my own defense, I was very tired. And as most parents know, fatigue is why we make rash decisions.

One such time was when Colton's fifth-grade trumpet section decided to wear white pants for a performance.

White pants for skinny teenage boys are not real plentiful. We'd proved this premise at about eight stores when exhaustion numbed the portion of my brain that has compassion for the skinny teen who was finding shoes he wanted to buy, shirts he really needed, and socks he would absolutely for sure pick up off the floor of his room if I bought them for him. With all the "good stuff" he was discovering, he seemed totally unconcerned about our lack of success in finding the original reason for our marathon shopping trip.

As he wandered off to look at yet more shoes which would markedly improve his athletic performance, I spied a sale rack with dozens of white pants. Carefully, I looked over my shoulder to make certain Colton didn't see me enter the girls' section of the department store.

I fingered the heavy denim and thought how perfect the fabric. I held a pair of pants up and realized these were an ideal length for him. I looked at the slim size and determined they probably wouldn't fall down while he stood to play a solo. I looked at the half-off price and decided what the kid didn't know wouldn't hurt him.

Carefully, in case I needed to reattach it, I pulled the pink price tag off and stuck it in my back pocket. Looking across the store, I made sure Colton was still engrossed in the various styles of basketball shoes.

Moving from the women's section to the men's, I hung the pants among the grey Dockers and then called to my son.

"Hey, I think I found a pair."

"Okay," he said watching me pull them from the men's rack. "Can I buy the shoes?"

"No. Go try the pants on."

"It doesn't matter," he said glancing at them. "They'll fit."

"No. You need to try these on," I said, wondering if the backside of this pair were for a teen girl or a mature woman.

Reluctantly he trailed off to the dressing room. He grumbled when I made him come out and model.

"Turn around," I said.

"Mom," he muttered as he pivoted and headed back to the dressing room.

I watched him walk away satisfied that the jeans appeared to be a skinny, no-butt teen girl fit.

My son was surprised when I encouraged him to go back and look at the shoes. But, I didn't want him to see the pink tag I took out of my back pocket for the cashier to scan.

We filmed his performance. He did great. I asked him how the pants worked.

"They're okay," he said. "We'll probably wear black pants next time though. White pants feel weird in the butt. Even Preston, the kid that plays second chair, said that."

I'm thinking Preston's mom gets tired too sometimes.

There are, of course, many incidents too embarrassing and stupid to write. I, like other mothers. live with extreme guilt. Horrible guilt. We wallow in it. We eat it for breakfast. But we adoptive mothers live with even more guilt. Would this child have been better in another home? Will he be ashamed of me when we meet, his birth mother and I. And guilt. It wraps us around and makes us angry. Not only do our children throw it in our faces, but unconsciously others do to. It's all around us.

My oldest was only twelve when Lorie, our 17-year-old neighbor, got pregnant. The physical tortures of pregnancy are incredible. I'm sorry she had to go through this physical and emotional trial. All around me those who knew of the situation sympathized and wanted to know how she could give up that child. They came to my home and asked me. They called about other matters and we all talked about the hard time Lorie was going through and how hard it is to "give up a baby."

Lorie cried after meeting the family she planned to place with.

Before going into labor, she talked with them. They were called and told she was in labor. Then communication ceased. They didn't know what was happening. Should they set up a crib? Can she go through with this? They waited. She cried. She gets to decide their future. She is in control of the baby's future. She feels out of control. A couple waited. They knew they were at her mercy. She felt helpless. She wanted the baby. They want the baby. Legally they could do nothing but wait. I felt for them. I've been them.

I like this birth mother. I'd known her a long time. I know her family. They are good people. They care about babies. For two days, I had no idea what she would do. Because of her pregnancy and relationship with our family, we've had some very blunt discussions in our house. My children were divided in their opinions of what our friend should do. None of them, however, mentioned the baby in their opinions. They talked of those other characters in this drama. The pregnant girl's little sister. The pregnant girl's new boyfriend. The girl's mother and father and how adoption would affect these people. None of my children mentioned the baby.

My children are typical of discussions involving adoption. How will adoption affect those around this situation? Seldom is the baby the 3-year-old this baby will turn into, the 10-year-old this child will become, the teenager this infant will grow into, these are not often discussed.

Once the baby was born my group of children were more considerate of this little one. Their responses, however, were still mixed.

"The baby probably wants to be adopted by someone richer than us."

"I think the baby should go to a family that lives in the country and has horses," said one who had been begging for a pony.

Adoption seemed fine to them when they just discussed the baby.

Adoption, even to my adopted children, was not fine when they considered the others involved because of the pain those others would feel. My children believe people should be adopted, but they don't believe families should release babies for adoption. And so I need to feel gratitude for the pain others endured on my behalf.

I used to get really tired of being grateful. I'd been grateful for so long, I'd brandished my gratitude every time we spoke about adoption. Grateful for the mothers who, like our neighbor, endured hardship for me. I've been reminded at least once a week since getting our first child how grateful I should be. I've been reminded how I failed at producing a child and so I have to endure ten years, twenty years, thirty years, a lifetime of gratitude. When does the statute of limitations end for groveling?

If the birth mother wants to send her parents to the legalization process at the courthouse, adoptive parents have to say, "Yes." If the birth family wants pictures for a year, adoptive family must jump on board. Pictures quarterly forever, "Sure no problem." Adoptive parents have to be compliant, because we were given something we could not get on our own, so we are to be grateful forever.

I used to be bothered by this. I'm not any more. I am so grateful for the birth mothers of my children. I've loved these biological mothers often and deeply, but it's a feeling that will swell at unsuspected times. When I'd see Alexis walk across the parking lot as I arrive to pick her up from drama. When I saw Garrett collapse under a scout pack. At these times, when I know how precious each life is, I often say a silent prayer of gratitude and ask for blessings upon the head of the one who made possible my blessing. I never feel the genuine gratitude when someone mentions to me how I owe this all to someone else.

I hope to hug all of my children's birthparents and personally tell them, "Thank you." I've had such an opportunity with my oldest daughter. We are different, this birthmother and myself. But we do agree on one thing. Our daughter is beautiful, and she got the best of both of us. What more can one want for a child?

Our 17-year-old friend and neighbor spent several days crying. People would ask, "How can anyone give up a child?" (Why are they asking me? Am I not the last person in the neighborhood to question?) I didn't mention this irony to them. But I did want to correct their speech. "Don't say give up a child." That sounds like failure. She's considering placing a child. That sounds like searching and finding a safe place to harbor a life. Yet, I couldn't say "finding the best place for the child." Such a statement would have suggested arrogance on my part. As if I knew our home was the best place for a baby.

When the baby was about 3 days old, Lorie's mother called. Said things weren't well. Lorie was reconsidering her decision. Another neighbor called. She can't believe anyone could even consider for a moment actually giving up a baby.

Most people don't believe in adoption. Oh, sure, as long as they don't hear me yell at my kids, then they think we should adopt, but few folks really believe children should be placed for adoption. They tell us that frequently. Which is your own child? Like the others are on loan until the real parents come to claim them.

After coming home from the hospital, Lorie didn't leave the house. She stayed home with the child she gave birth to. I knew she was still crying. I knew, even as the couple chosen to be the adoptive family traveled to our town, my neighbors were reconsidering. I knew the birth grandfather wanted to make certain this decision was right. I talked to my neighbors the night Lorie came home. I could have called the next morning. I could have asked how they felt knowing someone was coming intent to leave with this newborn. My friends wouldn't have resented my call. We are close. They've told me a lot. I don't know if they told me how they really felt. I adopted children. They would never tell me some things.

Four mornings after this tiny infant first squinted into the light, two vans were parked in front of my neighbor's house. I knew the family vehicle with out-of-state plates belonged to the adoptive parents. The other van belonged to my neighbors. I saw them load the baby into my neighbor's van. I saw doors slam on both vans. Lorie walked carefully and painfully, hurting from her recent C-section. The potential adoptive mother moved quickly, climbing into her own vehicle. The vans pulled out, driving up the road a discrete distance apart. I knew the original plan was to go to an attorney for relinquishment of the birth mother's rights. Maybe Lorie and her family finally felt comfortable placing the baby. How hard is this trip? But maybe they are only going to town and the potential adoptive family is going back to their home without a new baby. How hard is their trip?

A baby comes to earth. A child will be raised, bathed, held, and will learn to laugh. She will be told to eat supper before she can have a cookie. A little girl will grow out of that infant's body. She will have to decide whether she'll volunteer as a bell ringer at Christmas time or simply shop at the mall with her friends. She will hug, and cry, and have acne when she wants to look flawless. She will be snubbed by friends in sixth grade. She will hate all the clothes in her closet. She will cry because she's tired and doesn't want mother to put her to bed. Who is the mother that will put her to bed?

When I saw the two vans drive up the road, I cried. I don't know why. I was not involved in this child's future. Yet, I prayed the correct decision would be made, and I prayed the other woman would feel peace.

I prayed this would happen for every child from Heaven and for every woman who loves babies.

But, mostly I prayed for my children. Those in my home. Those black, those white. I prayed that I, their mother, can help them and I prayed that their other mothers, the birth mothers, feel peace. And I hope all these children can get the best from both moms.

Our oldest daughter has spent time with her birth family. Gone on trips, picnics and overnighters and she finds them fascinating. There is a simple reason for this. They find her fascinating. They listen to her with great intensity, soaking in every idiom, facial expression and curve of the lip.

We don't. We've seen them all before.

"What?" I said as she talked.

"They were so interested in what I have to say," she said again. "They were so amazed about my basketball stories."

"What stories?" I asked, trying to concentrate as I checked to see if her younger brother's own basketball schedule was posted online.

"About never losing a league game for over ten years." she said. "And our basketball trips, I told them about . . ."

I think she finished what she told them, I'm not sure because I had to call a woman who also has a son on my son's team and find out where the game was.

It's a good thing to find out who you look like and get to know those who are related to you biologically, but she's still our daughter. Who but us can ignore her and still love her? I plan to help all our children find their birth parents as soon as I'm not so frantic looking up athletic schedules and trying to earn enough money to pay their tuition.

I've heard speculative horror stories about the woes of adopted children. Additional coverage is given to minority children adopted by white couples. Yet actual studies of children fail to support these horrors.

Colton had me read an essay he was writing for a college English class. I plagiarized this next part from his paper. He may have plagiarized the quote from somewhere else. I don't know. He said in part:

"Critics claim adoption is not a 'solution' because it has potential problems. Children may be abused by adoptive parents, or feel second-class, or the birth mother may track down the child later and cause havoc. But there are no solutions in life. There are only trade-offs. There are problems in every situation. Adoption is a problem I can deal with."

Chapter 24

The fast food chain was next door to where Garrett worked. We stopped to meet him for a quick lunch. The food was marginal, but it was fun to see our son who was living ten hours away.

When the diner at the table next to us flopped to the floor and started convulsing, most of us were too surprised to react. Garrett, however, dropped to one knee, leaned over to keep the man's head from pounding against a table leg.

Fries and unchewed food spewed over Garrett's fingers as the convulsions continued unabated. Other customers moved forward and someone reached down and found the chain around the unconscious man's neck. The medical alert tag read, "Epileptic."

"I'll call 911," a man said.

Garrett sustained the drooling head while the grand mal seizure continued. As the man's muscles started to relax, sirens screamed into the parking lot. EMTs with gloves and face masks replaced Garrett.

My brother has seizures so Garrett was familiar with what might happen. This was one of the reasons he could respond so quickly and compassionately. In recounting the occurrence, Garrett would later describe the man by his nationality and age. Because Garrett sees color. He's not "color blind" like a neighbor bragged to me one day.

"I don't even notice the color of their skin," she said. "I'm color blind."

Well, Garrett did see the color of the unconscious man's skin, but this color remained irrelevant. Garrett has the type of personality who quickly comes to another's aid. Certainly, there would have been others in the restaurant. As a society we are incredibly caring during a crisis. I was just grateful that there was no unconscious bias in Garrett which would have caused him to hesitate before offering assistance.

Bias is when you have a little bit of an "ick" factor before getting that close to someone so unlike yourself. (Although half-chewed fries are "ick" from anyone.)

Bias is when you're willing to have Colton join your family for water skiing, but he can't ride on the tube with your daughter because he'll either be aggressive with her or will take risks with the boat.

When Michael Brown, an unarmed black teenager, was shot and killed in Ferguson, Missouri, a serious of protests rocked the area for weeks. Colton and his friend, Nicole, were in the living room discussing the incident.

Nicole is blond and white and she was disgusted the officer hadn't been indicted by the grand jury.

"Cops are prejudiced," Nicole said passionately. She was angry about Ferguson police shooting a man and then allowing him to lie in his own blood. "I've known cops," she continued. "I've heard them talk."

The 20-year-old was raised by an attorney. She probably had heard cops. She was sure Michael Brown's death was racially motivated.

Whether her vehement stance was part of her personality--a tendency to care for the underdog--or whether she had been swayed by hearing a police officer speak disrespectfully of blacks, I cannot say. I imagine both propensities are involved.

Colton, who always has an opinion, was much less critical. He wasn't so certain the act could be called racially motivated. Granted his nature is to see both sides of an issue, and he is often prepared to play devil's advocate after finding out what the other person in the room believes. But also, Colton has lived with and around whites who would never hurt him.

"I'd have shot, too, if someone reached into my vehicle," he said.

More than personality was involved in these two varied opinions. Nicole had heard whites disrespect other races. Certainly, Colton has, too; however, he has lived with love from whites.

Certainly, he wasn't as worried about his safety as I was that February night when he called me disoriented and confused.

Exactly how Colton got home after hitting the barrier is a little unclear. He apparently changed the tire, drove four miles down a major street and pulled into his aunt's driveway. How he accomplished this feat without help is vague. Maybe he had help: divine intervention, muscle memory, pure luck.

My sister, after asserting how limited his reasoning powers were, decided an emergency room visit would be advisable. Confused and disoriented, still, he was cognizant enough to take his blanket. For Christmas I had made him a queen-sized covering out of his favorite material. He used the gift regularly for sleeping, lounging and running out to his car before he got dressed in the morning. Because the quilt was so extremely useful and versatile, I think I'm safe to say there had never been a convenient time to laundry the item. Certainly, the emergency room staff would understand. They didn't.

Two things happened soon after his arrival. The staff took his blanket and the staff decided to test him for drugs. A nurse, concerned with cleanliness and germs, started down the hall, holding the blanket at arm's length. The injured boy sprang from his bed and accused the woman of stealing his "stuff." He tried to wrestle the beloved item from her. The fact he was chasing medical personnel down the hall and begging for his blanket, may have added to the staff's insistence a drug test be administered forthwith.

"That's the second time I've passed a drug test," he told me later in the week. We were talking on the phone. His fever had subsided and his concussion headache was mostly gone.

"What?" I asked him.

"The last time you had me drug tested I was clean," he bragged. "And this time, too."

Neither of us thought to imply the drug test had been racially motivated. Chasing a nurse down the hall with your backside hanging out of the hospital gown kind of suggests a need for a few scientific screenings.

"Yeah, I know," he laughed. "But it's still your fault. 'Cause you gave me that blanket."

Wrapped in the Christmas present I made for him, Colton left the hospital several hours after being pronounced drug free. I wasn't there. I'm seldom there for him now. Yet I walked with him in snake grass and drove six hours to watch him run a 100-yard dash .01 seconds slower than the other guy. I've laid awake all night listening for his Honda. I hid tears when I knew he didn't want my sympathy.

He's a Marine. He can change a tire while burning up with fever and suffering a traumatic brain injury. What can his mother possibly do for him now?

Any child-raising arrogance I possessed is long gone. It seeped away slowly during so many confusing moments of not knowing. But the selfishness remains, so grateful for the honor to mother them—Black and White.

About the Author

Teaching is a way of life for ViAnn. She has taught high school English, journalism, special education and YIC (Youth in Custody). Eventually, she decided to teach part time as an adjunct professor, so she could spend more time with her children.

After welcoming their third child, a high maintenance little boy who cried and tore at his own skin, she decided to stay home for a while. The while turned into 20 years and two more children. From home she has written weekly columns and feature stories while trying to help her children, black and white, maneuver through a complicated world.

To see more of ViAnn, check out her website at

http://www.krpublishing.org/

Follow our blog or go to our website at
http://www.krpublishing.org/

If you have any other thoughts, comments or ideas, feel free to post them on our website in the link above.

www.ingramcontent.com/pod-product-compliance
Lightning Source LLC
Chambersburg PA
CBHW061730020426
42331CB00006B/1176

* 9 7 8 0 6 9 2 6 2 2 9 3 3 *